THE WI CREATIVE GUIDE TO Machine Embroidery

ENID GRATTAN-GUINNESS

UNWIN

HYMAN

To my husband Ivor I lovingly dedicate this book

First published in Great Britain by Unwin Hyman, an
imprint of Unwin Hyman Limited, 1988.
© Enid Grattan-Guinness 1988

UNWIN HYMAN LIMITED
15/17 Broadwick Street
London
W1V 1FP

and

Allen & Unwin Australia Pty Ltd
8 Napier Street, North Sydney, NSW 2060, Australia

Allen & Unwin New Zealand PTY Ltd with the Port
Nicholson Press, 60 Cambridge Terrace, Wellington, New
Zealand

British Library Cataloguing in Publication Data
Grattan-Guinness, Enid
  The WI guide to creative machine
  embroidery.
  1. Embroidery, Machine
  I. Title
  746.44'028   TS1783

  ISBN 0-04-440129-9

Photography by Steve Tanner
Line artwork by Jil Shipley

Designed by Colin Lewis and Associates
Typeset by Latimer Trend & Company Ltd, Plymouth
Printed in Portugal by
Printer Portuguesa, Sintra

CONTENTS

INTRODUCTION

'Birdy I' by Joy Clucas

Let me say straight away that you don't need a sewing machine with numerous fancy stitches for this embroidery. As long as your machine sews straight and zigzag or satin stitch, that's all you'll need. Even if your machine only sews straight, you can still get a great deal of enjoyment out of this book.

Then let me say that it doesn't damage or mess your machine up at all! Mine is 16 years old and hasn't broken down yet, and I do all the usual dressmaking on it as well.

To many people this embroidery will come as a complete surprise, as they might never have seen it before, or didn't realise that their machines could be so versatile and do such things. This new approach to embroidery has developed with the sewing machine, becoming a highly individual craft which allows great freedom to those who wish it, while the more traditionally minded embroidress will have the comfort of making full use of familiar skills. It also has the advantage of speed over hand sewing, for busy Mums, Grannies and Aunts.

The beauty of this embroidery is that it can be very durable; the little dress in the project on page 78 was washed in the washing machine at least once a week for 20 months, and is as you now see it. However, the craft can be used to create very delicate embroideries, depending on the fabrics, threads or techniques used.

Don't worry if you can't immediately find any of the machine embroidery threads mentioned throughout the book, just start with what you have until you can buy some. There is a good list of suppliers at the end of the book.

The book is written to lead you step by step through the simplest embroidery, and on to more challenging techniques. The Projects are designed to do the same; you won't have to work through the whole book before you can have a go at one, just work through to the end of Chapter 3 and then try the easy ones. The Projects are there not only to give you practice but also to give you ideas which can be expanded once the techniques are at your fingertips. But just like any new craft, it does need application, don't be downhearted if your first efforts don't look like the pictures, they very soon *will* look like them if you have a go and do a bit of practice.

Use machine embroidery on clothes, coffee and tea cosies, tissue box covers, cushion covers, table cloths, bed linen, mounted pictures, all sorts of ecclesiastical items, and so on. Once you have started, you just won't want to stop!

CHAPTER ONE

An Introduction to Your Machine

FIRST THINGS FIRST

It's free and fast

Creative embroidery on your sewing machine is a very immediate craft form: it grows quickly, and allows great freedom. I will admit that it feels strange at first—but my students describe the feeling when they first get sewing as fun, fascinating or even liberating!

Any machine can do it

Creative embroidery can be done on practically any domestic swing-needle sewing machine (that is where the needle swings from side to side to sew zigzag), even the simplest; it isn't necessary to have lots of built-in fancy stitches. The domestic swing-needle machines first came on the market in the mid-1950s, so there must be an enormous group of owners who have no idea what beautiful things can be done with the very same machines on which they make their curtains and sew their dresses.

It is not a difficult craft to master, and by the time you have worked through this book you will be surprised, and I hope delighted, at the ability you have so quickly developed.

Swing-needle or straight sewing

The book is designed for the owners of a swing-needle machine—although don't despair if yours only sews straight, you can still get a lot out of this book. In fact there is some exquisite embroidery done on treadle machines which dates way back to the 1880s and it was probably being done before then. Remember the domestic swing-needle machine did not come on the market until 70 years later.

It is assumed:
- That you own a domestic swing-needle machine.
- That you know how to thread it up, and how to wind and insert a bobbin.
- That you have some practical experience in using it, can sew a straight seam and have a working knowledge of how to make the machine sew zigzag and satin stitch.
- That you have looked in your machine handbook and have an idea how to set up the machine for darning or free embroidery. (*Don't panic* if you lost the book years ago, never had it, or the dog ate it, all will be revealed anon!)

Fools rush in!

I know the temptation is to dip into a craft book where it looks attractive, and have a go—I do it myself—but in this case, do try to be strong willed and resist. DON'T be tempted to turn straight to the chapter that tells you how to sew a certain stitch, unless you have already had some lessons.

This book is written so that, if you read it from the beginning, with your machine in front of you, neither you nor your machine will suffer. You should end up with a good working knowledge of the basics of creative embroidery and perhaps a better working knowledge of your sewing machine which will save a lot of fury and frustration and that blue cloud that sits over your head when your sewing won't go right!

A QUICK TOUR OF YOUR SEWING MACHINE

The drawing shows a typical sewing machine, labelled with the various parts that will be mentioned from time to time throughout the book. Check them against your own machine so that we are all talking the same language.

To thread the *top thread* , the spool or reel of thread sits on the *spool pin* (A) runs through a *thread guide/s* (B) to the *tension discs* (C) (these sit on the front of my machine, but they could be tucked away inside the top of yours) from the tension discs to the *take-up lever* (D) (that's the lever that goes up and down almost in time with your needle) and down through one or two more thread guides and into your *needle* (E).

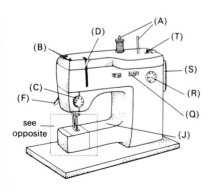

see opposite

The *presser bar lever* (F) is just at the back of the busy end of your machine, it raises and lowers the *presser bar* (G) which has attached to its end your *presser foot* (H).

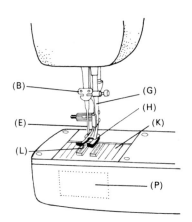

- This is a really important lever, because it also controls the tension in your top thread, and it is only when this lever is down that the top thread is under tension and your machine will sew properly. See ●● below.

In the *bed* (J) of your machine, just where the needle goes in, is a removable part called the *needle plate* (K), and in the middle of this are the parts that move the fabric along under the presser foot, called the *feed dogs* (L) (you may know them as the teeth).

Under the *needle plate* is the bobbin race with its *rotary hook* (M) (in your machine it may oscillate, or move back and forth) which whizzes round the *bobbin case* (N) which is sometimes fixed and sometimes removable, and which contains the *bobbin* (P). See ●●● below.

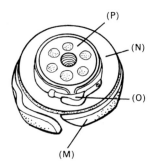

- ●● Once threaded through the *tension spring* (O), the bobbin is always under tension.

Other parts are: *stitch width lever* (Q) (yours may be a knob), *stitch length knob* (R) (yours may be a lever), *flywheel,* (S) which gives control of the needle movement by hand and is often released when the *bobbin winder* (T) is used.

HOW A STITCH IS MADE

- ●●● You may not see any point in knowing how stiches are made, but in creative embroidery knowledge is wisdom, and this knowledge will save you heartache and furious frustration! By understanding what goes on under the needle plate, you learn what goes right, and how to put right what goes wrong!

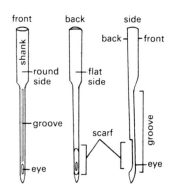

Once you have read and understood this, then watch your own machine working. The drawing shows several views of a machine needle.

When a needle is threaded, the thread comes down the front of the needle to the eye, and when the needle goes

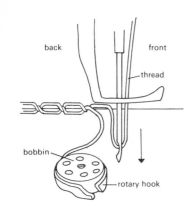

through the fabric the thread tucks itself neatly away in the long groove and so saves itself from wear and tear by friction against the fabric. The indentation behind the eye, called the scarf, is there to allow the needle to sit more snugly next to the rotary hook.

After lowering the presser bar lever (F) to put the top thread under tension, the needle goes down into the fabric.

A little loop of top thread is formed as the needle starts to come out. The rotary hook (M) whizzes round the bobbin race and nips into the loop.

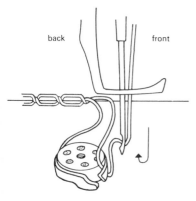

It takes the loop of top thread round the stationary bobbin thread, making them twist round each other to make a stitch.

The needle comes out of the fabric, the take-up lever (D) takes up the slack thread, and the top tension discs (C) allow just enough thread through for the stitch.

- The stitch is only complete when the needle is at its highest point out of the fabric. The take-up lever will be on its way down again. Now the process can begin again.

Now watch how your machine does it _but_:
- Hold on to both threads as you do it. Turn the fly-wheel (S) gently, and don't use the motor.
- If you don't put the presser bar lever down the thread may not come out cleanly, which will result in a lot of loose looping under your embroidery, or the top thread will become wound round the bobbin case and disaster!
  _or_
  the fabric will lift up with the needle and the thread will loop too high so that the rotary hook whizzes round catching nothing in particular, resulting in a skipped stitch.

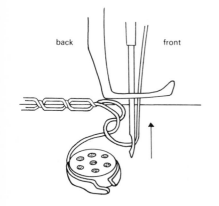

ALL ABOUT BOBBINS

Make sure that you have the correct bobbin for your machine.
There is only one way to wind a bobbin—and to judge from some of the efforts of my students, not everybody

knows it! Check through the following to ensure that you are getting it right.

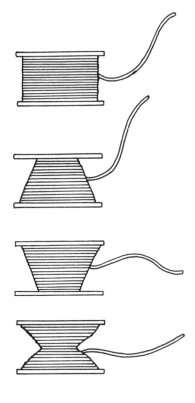

- Your bobbin should be wound as neatly as a reel of thread.
- Bottom heavy bobbins: the thread will just pull too easily off.
- Top heavy bobbins: the thread will pull off under the added tension of the overhang, sometimes even getting embedded in it!
- 'Sexy' bobbins: you get both problems at once—pull and tug!
- Your bobbin tension will be wrong if the bobbin is not wound correctly. Before you start, remove all thread from a bobbin before winding on fresh or the newly wound thread will sink into the soft thread already there and will not run off properly.

Winding a bobbin

If there is a hole in the top of your bobbin, thread your cotton through it. When you start winding, hold on to the thread until it is firmed in then stop and cut off the tail. Continue winding. if your machine doesn't wind neatly, you just have to help it with a little guidance.

- If you insert the bobbin and leave the tail flying, the needle may catch it while you are sewing—which will then play havoc with everything else that is whizzing and zooming under the needle plate.

Bobbins into cases

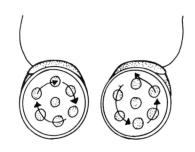

If your thread goes through your bobbin tension spring to the left, your bobbin must fit into the case winding clockwise. If your thread goes through your bobbin tension spring to the right, your bobbin must fit into the case winding anti-clockwise. Check this out with your machine handbook.

- Your bobbin tension will be wrong if the bobbin is put in upside-down.

UNDER TENSION

Now we know (or knew already anyway) that there are three sets of tensions to make a stitch:

1. Top thread tension, through the tension discs; under tension *only* when the presser bar lever is down.
2. Bobbin thread tension through its tension spring; always under tension once threaded through the spring.
3. Fabric tension, made by the presser foot against the feed dogs.

Altering your top tension

As you work through the book you will find that the top tension will need to be altered. Check in your handbook to see how this is done if you are not sure. If your tension disc knob is not graded by numbers, try and mark it somehow, where it is at balanced tension for seam stitching, so that you can always go straight back to it.

● The reason for loosening the top thread tension is because it is set for sewing hems, and holding fabrics firmly together. To get the thread to lie smoothly in embroidery, and to stop it from breaking when under the pressure of fast or strong movements of the hoop, it is loosened off. It will also pucker the fabric less in solid cover embroidery. How much to loosen it will depend entirely on your sewing machine. For instance, my top tension is marked 1–9, with 5 as the balanced tension, and I loosen mine off to 3, occasionally less.

Note: Alteration of the bobbin tension is not covered in this book.

CHAPTER TWO
Important Information Before Starting

Machine cleaning

Before you start sewing make sure you have cleaned out all the lint, fluff and odd bits of cotton from under your needle plate and around the bobbin. If your machine needs oiling check in your handbook to see if the bobbin race should also be oiled.

TO START YOU WILL NEED:

Fabric—even weave, smooth and unpatterned
Needles—a packet of 90/14 to suit your machine
Thread—30 or 50 machine embroidery
Hoops—for embroidery, wooden and adjustable
Scissors—small and sharp-ended
Seam ripper—optional but useful

FABRICS

The ideal fabric is a firm fabric, that has very little or no stretch in either grain. To start with, the outer edges of old sheets that are not worn are good, especially plain ones, provided they don't stretch too much.

When buying fabric to use on a project, as well as a firm fabric choose a plain, even weave one, unless you want to include the pattern or texture in your design.

Furnishing or dress fabrics are ideal and remember that your choice doesn't have to be cotton, it could be nylon, rayon, organza, curtain nets or even vegetable nets; you can be quite experimental.

- Always give prospective fabric the stretch test. If it stretches beyond a small amount it will never tighten properly in the hoop, and once embroidered upon, will pucker when taken out of the hoop.
- Beware also of twill and satin weaves, where the threads can pull in an ugly fashion, or swallow your stitches.

NEEDLES

90/14 needles are the best to use for all embroidery, (unless a thicker one is indicated) and can happily be used on even the finest materials. The needle is often under great tension when machine embroidering, and the narrower ones break too often. Mind you, you will probably even break a 90/14! Don't worry, just change it. You break them less often the more proficient you become.

Always use a new needle for each new project (or several tiny projects). *Never* use a blunt needle.

Remember, the front of the needle has the long groove and round top.

- Make sure you only use those needles recommended for your sewing machine. They do differ, and the wrong ones can be the cause of your machine skipping stitches and not sewing properly.

THREADS

If you can find it, machine embroidery thread is obviously perfect for this work. I always start my students on 50 machine embroidery cotton as this is the very finest, and once they can manage that, they can handle anything! All of the examples in this book were done with DMC 50 machine embroidery cotton (which is very fine) and some Madeira metallic threads simply because that is what I happen to have come across in my time as a machine embroidress. However, any of the following threads can be used with equal success: DMC 50 (fine) and 30 (less fine) cotton, Anchor 50 and 30 cotton, Madeira Metallic and 40 Rayon thread and Natesh titania rayon. Madeira and Natesh have a silky sheen. They all come in reels varying from 200m to 500m, and are obviously going to be more expensive than a reel of ordinary cotton which only has 100m on it. If you are unable to find any embroidery thread locally, look at the suppliers list at the end of the book. It is possible to find other more exotic threads, and some pretty, but ordinary weight ones. Find what you can to start with, and then build up your collection.

If you cannot get machine embroidery thread, then certainly use any of the threads that you have available, but do take care as some of the man-made fibres have a built-in stretch.

- Be careful which embroidery thread you use on which fabric; rayon thread will not take a hot iron, so use with care on cotton garments.

If you have had your cotton for a long time, it may lose its colour and go dry and brittle. Either keep it in a less drying atmosphere, or waste the cotton round the outside. Joy Clucas, my teacher, suggests steaming it on a rack over boiling water while Robbie Fanning in her book on machine embroidery, prefers to leave it out all night in the dew or to give it a fine water spray!

ALL ABOUT HOOPS

Why a hoop?
To put creative in creative machine embroidery, you must have freedom of movement—you won't have this if all the time your presser foot is holding the fabric firmly down against the feed dogs. So, remove the foot, and replace the lost tension in the fabric by stretching it in a hoop. (No, don't take off your presser foot yet!)

What sort of hoop?
The hoop must be narrow (about 1cm, $\frac{3}{8}$ in) to fit under your machine needle at its highest point. It must have an adjustable screw. A good size to start with is 20cm, 8in or 23cm, 9in diameter. I have a whole family of them now, but find I use the 25cm, 10in–30cm, 12in sizes most as they save re-hooping so often to fit the design in. The inner hoop must be bound with bias binding or tape, which holds the sewing fabric more firmly, and prevents it from marking, as in the photograph on page 13.

STRETCHING THE FABRIC IN YOUR HOOP

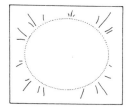

- **Very important**: Unless your fabric is properly stretched in your hoop, your embroidery will never look or sit right. The embroidery frame is also called a Tambour frame—a tambour is a little drum. So when your fabric is properly stretched in your hoop it must be 'drum tight', and ping with quite a high tone when flicked.

Having bound your inner hoop with care, put both hoops together and tighten the screw as tightly as you comfortably can with your fingers.

Stand at your table, put the outer hoop on the table; and smoothly lay the fabric over the top of it.

Fit the inner hoop into the outer, on the side furthest away from you. Controlling the inner hoop with your fingers, push the nearest side into place with a sharp shove of the heels of your hands. If at first you don't succeed . . .

- I have always been told that if you can get the hoops in while sitting down, they will be too loose.

Take up a soft pleat of fabric in both hands with thumb and finger, just above the edge of the hoop *nearest* to you. Keeping your hands close together, pull the fabric up and over the inner hoop and away from you. Use the remaining fingers as a brace against the inner hoop.

- In this way you will be tightening the fabric and keeping the inner hoop in place at the same time.

Turn the hoop and repeat the process, keeping your hands close together, until the fabric is 'drum tight'.

Whilst tightening the fabric, make sure that the grain lines are kept straight.

- If the grain line is bent and then embroidered over, it will straighten when taken out of the hoop and your work will distort.

To remove the inner hoop, just pop it out, don't loosen the screw. If the hoops are so tight that you can't pull the fabric, loosen the screw a little bit. If it loses its drum-tightness easily, tighten the screw again until it holds.

- Remember that if your fabric is too loose it will be taken upwards by the needle and won't make a stitch.

ARE YOU SITTING COMFORTABLY?

When sewing creatively, you will find yourself sitting for long concentrated periods, so you must find the most comfortable way to sit to avoid neck ache, shoulder ache or arm ache.

Place your machine directly in front of you, with work space to the left. Your work should be bust height, and your needle slightly to the right. Rest your left elbow on the table and left hand on the edge of the machine bed. Your chair should be pulled well in for good back support. Your right hand and arm do most of the work, the left hand being used for fine control. Keep your right elbow relaxed.

Are you having to lean down to see your work? Are you close enough to the machine? If you have an ache, always find the cause and do something about it.

SETTING UP YOUR MACHINE FOR CREATIVE EMBROIDERY

There should be a section in your machine handbook which tells you how to set it up for darning or free embroidery. Follow those instructions for best results. However, if you don't have your handbook, I shall go through the steps one by one anyway. Check these steps with your book too, if you have it.

Remove presser foot and/or foot clip from the presser bar, leaving it quite naked.

- Make a habit of putting these straight into your accessory box to avoid them being accidentally swept up with all the unwanted bits on your sewing table.

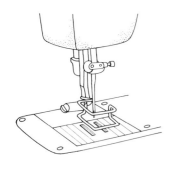

My machine has a neat finger protector for embroidery, which is a good thing to have for a beginner. Try and find out if you can get one for your machine.

Put in a new 90/14 needle. The long groove and round top are the front.

Cover (in my case) or lower your feed dogs, or slip in or put on the special needle plate—whatever your handbook says. You don't want to have your dogs leaping up and down under your work. If your machine does none of these things, then you'll just have to get used to the slight movement and take it into account when using fine fabrics.

Position the stitch length knob at 0 and stitch width lever at 0, (see R + Q page 8).

- The occasional machine prefers to have a small amount of stitch length.

If your tensions have been altered from previous sewing, put them back to normal.

If your machine has an extension table, to give you a wider area on which to sew, you will need it. If you only have the narrow bed of your machine, you will get more control over your hoop if you can improvise an extension sewing table from an old box file or some such.

Discover what *your* darning foot looks like, and keep it handy—it may be that your machine will only perform while it is attached.

a typical darning foot

THE LAST FEW, BUT IMPORTANT THINGS

Safety
When you start machine embroidery, **keep your fingers and hands at the edge of the hoop and away from the unprotected needle.**

Fluff brush
Brush out the fluff and lint from under the needle plate after each day's embroidery, ready for next time. Check that there is no cotton caught round the bobbin race from a previous disaster.

Oiling
Keep an ear and eye on the need to oil your machine (if it is the sort that needs oiling by you), especially the bobbin race. Check with your handbook.

With much older machines, make sure its engine does not overheat, it may need a touch of engine grease every now and then.

CHAPTER THREE

making a Start

PART ONE Free Hand Straight Sewing

It will be difficult for you to follow these instructions unless you have read Chapters 1 and 2. Even if you have already undergone a series of machine embroidery lessons, it is important to check through the first two chapters before going ahead with this one.

PRACTICE WITHOUT THREADS— A TOE IN THE WATER

Set your machine up as on page 18 but don't thread it up—either top or bobbin. Put the fabric in the hoop as explained on pages 16 and 17. Check your chair, table and machine for comfort. Stitch length 0, stitch width 0.

HOOPS AGAIN

Put the presser bar lever up, (see page 9) and raise the needle as high as it will go, by moving the flywheel by hand. Slip the hoop under the needle, pressing down hard on the ring edge if necessary. Whatever you do, *don't bend the needle* while you are doing this. If it really will not go under, then just release the needle for a moment (this can be done whether it is threaded or not).

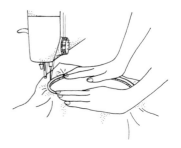

- The stretched fabric in the hoop must lie flush with the bed of the machine. You should see the whole of the inner hoop.
- Make sure that none of the edge fabric is folded under the hoop.

Presser bar lever down
Needle lowered into fabric
Left hand resting on hoop EDGE and elbow resting on table
Right hand holding hoop as in picture
Right elbow relaxed

INVISIBLE SEWING

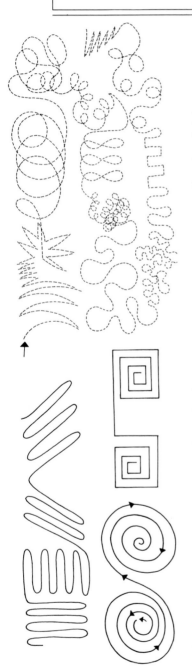

- If, now that you see it all set up, you are wary of that naked needle, put on the darning foot until you feel more confident. **Keep both hands out to the edge of your hoop**.

Hold and guide the hoop with your right hand, and steady it with your left.

With gentle but steady pressure on the foot pedal, start to move the hoop as soon as the needle moves. Keep the frame flat on the bed. Don't let it lift up.

Get used to moving your hoop: backwards and forwards in long sweeping movements and short sharp movements.

Swirl the hoop round in circles or twiddle it in tiny circles. Swirling the hoop will sew a circle, don't turn it from hand to hand as if you were driving a car!

Sew figures of eight, and sinuous serpentine bends as in the drawings shown.
The whole of this exercise is done by moving the hoop backwards, forwards and sideways and by swirling it round. The position of the hoop in your hands doesn't alter.

Now run the machine faster until it is running at full speed, and move your hoop more quickly.

Then run the machine slower until it is running as slow as possible, and move the hoop more slowly.
Continue the exercise until you feel more confident.

- If the needle seems to pull against, or pluck at, the fabric, this means that you are probably running the machine too slowly for the speed at which you are moving your hoop.

Draw or trace these shapes onto your fabric with a very hard pencil, or onto a piece of paper and pin that to your fabric (on whichever side is more convenient). Sew round them all several times, trying to follow the lines exactly. Don't turn the hoop from hand to hand, sew with continuous movement, even for the squares.

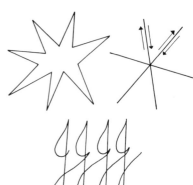

Go round each shape several times until you start to get the knack of keeping with the lines. Continue sewing until you feel the hoop moving quite smoothly at all speeds.

- If you feel the feed dogs moving under the fabric, have you remembered to lower or cover them?

SEWING WITH A THREAD— JUMPING IN WITH BOTH FEET

When you have had a good go at invisible sewing, thread up your machine with the same type of cotton top and bobbin, but in contrasting colours—50 machine embroidery cotton if possible. Remember, the top thread always sews the front of the work.

FOUR IMPORTANT THINGS

- Always pull up your bottom thread before you start sewing. Hold the top thread out to the side, turn the flywheel one turn and as the needle comes up and out of the fabric, pull the thread up and out to the side bringing the bobbin thread with it. The thread won't pull through until you have completed your stitch, with the needle at its highest point.

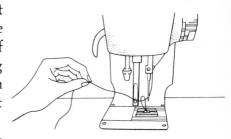

- Always lower the presser bar lever, to put tension on your top thread. If you don't do this, the stitches will be too loose or, worse, you'll get a nasty tangle of threads under your work and round the bobbin case.

    Should the worst happen (and it has happened numerous times to me), raise the needle to its highest point, or as high as you can, release and remove the hoop by cutting the mess under the hoop if necessary. Tidy your hoop, and make sure *all* the cotton is out from around the bobbin case. Say 'Bother' and remember to lower the pressure bar lever next time!

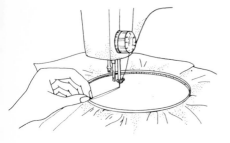

- Always lower the needle into the hoop at your starting point, and sew from there. It is practically impossible to aim from a raised needle position, and you can break your top thread.
- Hold onto both threads when you start sewing until they are firmed in with a few stitches, otherwise the top thread can get taken down and round the bobbin case—with a similar result to not lowering the presser bar lever. When firmed in they can just be left, or cut off.

Say to yourself every time you start to sew, until it becomes a habit, these Four Important Things:
'Pull up the bobbin thread
Lower the presser bar lever
Lower the needle into the fabric
Hold onto the threads'
If, when you try to start sewing, your machine just will not sew at all, or is obviously doing nasty things when you have tried a couple of times without a darning foot, stop immediately, put on your foot, and all should be well, (although your visibility will be hampered).

NOW TO BEGIN

With stitch length 0, stitch width 0, top tension normal, same thread top and bobbin but in contrasting colour, make sure the fabric is flush with the needle plate. You should see the whole of your inner hoop. Be sure no fabric is caught under the hoop.

Keeping your hands out to the edge of the hoop and remembering to hold onto both threads, start to sew just as you did without a thread. Move the hoop as the needle moves, but gently. It's rather like drawing by moving the paper not the pencil! *Always* keep the hoop and fabric pressed against the machine bed, don't let it lift up.

Repeat the exercises you have just done without a thread.

Your aim is smooth movement with both foot pedal and hoop. Remember you have free movement and swirl your hoop round, don't use it as a steering wheel.

- Don't be afraid to make your machine work. Run it fast—faster than if you were sewing a seam. Don't be tentative!

To move from one part of the hoop to another when sewing: raise the needle to its highest point (to finish the stitch), raise the presser bar lever, move to exactly where you want to start sewing, insert needle, lower presser bar, and start sewing. The bobbin cotton will remain under tension. If, however, you go too far and come back, you will have to pull up the bobbin thread, as it will have lost its tension.

- In your anxiety, you are almost certain to move the hoop too sharply at some point and *break the top thread*. Just thread it up and begin again. If it continues see page 26.
- You may *break a needle*—you will have pulled the hoop suddenly, just as the needle was going into the fabric, and pulled it off course enough to hit the needle plate and miss the hole. Just put in another needle!

Fill your hoop with movement practice, getting ideas from the colour plate on page 20. Become used to moving your hoop at the same time as running the machine. Run it fast and slowly, and move the hoop fast and slowly, as in invisible sewing.

Reproduce the patterns in the colour plate, then try and extend them, or invent some new ones of your own.

Note: It is perfectly acceptable to re-hoop over work already done.

When you have filled a couple of hoops with a variety of doodles have a break. Are you still sitting comfortably? Have a look at your work: see how the long stitches shine out and show up, and how the small stitches disappear. Notice how the bobbin thread comes up sometimes—this can often be used to very good effect. The lighter thread in your bobbin gives the work a translucent look, and a darker thread adds depth.

- Never throw away any practice piece until you know you won't need it again.

PROBLEM SOLVERS

Have you lowered your presser bar lever? This will be the answer to a lot of problems.

Is your hoop upside down? The fabric must be flush with the needle plate, and you must be able to see the whole of your inner hoop.

The top thread keeps breaking

Loosen the top thread tension little by little until it stops. (Check in your handbook how to do this if you don't already know.)

Re-thread the top thread.

Joggle the presser bar lever up and down, the discs sometimes stick.

Perhaps your thread is dry and brittle (see page 15). Change the thread, or waste the top layer of the reel.

Make sure there is no thread caught round your bobbin race from a previous disaster.

Bad bobbin thread stitching

Is your bobbin wound, threaded and inserted correctly? (See page 11 and check in your handbook.)

Is the bobbin race clear of cotton from a previous disaster?

Skipped stitches

Is the fabric in your hoop really drum tight? (See page 16).

Check your needle. Is it blunt, inserted wrongly or the wrong sort of needle for your machine? (See page 14 and check in your handbook.)

● Learn to stop immediately you hear something going wrong, and investigate. Like most problems, it almost certainly won't go away by itself!

PART TWO Free-Hand Zigzag and Satin Stitch

What is the difference? The difference between zigzag and satin stitch is that satin stitch is the closed-up version of zigzag, and has a continuous smoothly oversewn line. Zigzag is the opened-out version of satin stitch.

zigzag   satin stitch

SEWING FREE-HAND

Set up your machine, (see page 18), put your fabric in the hoop, (see page 16) and make sure you're sitting comfortably, (see page 17). Stitch length 0, stitch width 1–4, top tension normal to loose, same threads top and bobbin, in 2 contrasting colours, 50 embroidery thread if you can get it. Say to yourself, and do, the Four Important Things (from page 24):
'Pull up the bobbin thread
Lower the presser bar lever
Lower the needle into the fabric
Hold on to both threads'

NOW BEGIN

If there has been even a short break of time between one sewing session and the next, you may find a little practice is necessary to get your eye in again.

Before setting your stitch width lever, firm in your thread with a few stitches. Set the stitch width lever at its widest (mine is 4).

Keeping your hands out to the edge of the hoop start to sew just as you did for straight sewing, following the instructions from page 24, but using various widths of zigzag and satin stitch.

- Satin stitch is made by moving the hoop very slowly and running the machine quite quickly.

When you have filled a couple of hoops with movement practice, reproduce the textures and stitch patterns on page 28, then try to extend them, or invent some of your own.

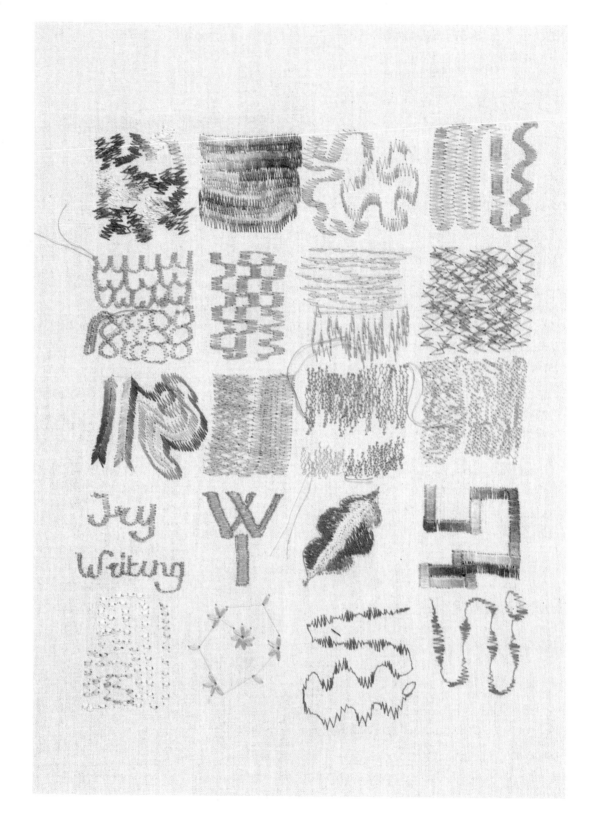

'Atom' by Joy Clucas

RUNNING STITCH WIDTH CONTROL

There are examples of this on the colour plate above. Hold your hoop at the edge with one hand (which hand depends on you) and work the stitch width control with the other. As you start to sew, move the hoop and the stitch width controls at the same time. In this way you can do patterns, and it will also help you to sew a controlled graded satin stitch when needed.

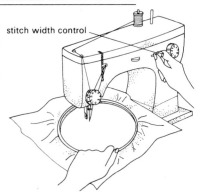

stitch width control

SATIN STITCH BLOBS

There are examples of these on the colour plate above. Stitch length 0, stitch width 4 to start, but any width, top tension normal to looser. Threads 50 embroidery if possible. If not, whatever you have available. Same colour top and bobbin.

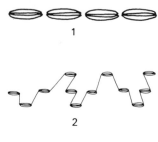

1

2

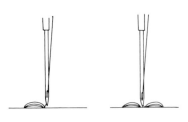

3

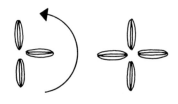

4

Presser bar lever down, firm in your stitch and needle down into starting point.

Hold the hoop very firmly by pressing down hard at the edges with both hands so that it *does not move*. Put your foot firmly down on the foot pedal and run the machine fast, (not tick-tick-tick, but brrrrrrr). Hold it down until a nice blob has been sewn.

To make patterns:

1. Sew a blob ending on the right hand side. Raise needle to highest point, (turn flywheel towards you) and move work to left. Lower the needle into the right hand side of the blob (turn flywheel towards you). Sew the next blob. 'Atom' by Joy Clucas on page 29 uses this technique.

2. As for 1, but move the work the planned distance in between each blob by raising presser bar lever (to relieve upper tension), make the move, needle down into fabric in planned spot, presser bar down, sew next blob.

3. Sew a blob with the needle ending *in* the right hand side. Turn the hoop on the needle so that the next blob will be sewn in the opposite direction, ending with the needle in the middle. Turn the hoop half round and sew a blob, ending with the needle in the middle. Turn in the opposite direction and sew another blob. Go on building up your star shape. The project on page 84 uses this technique.

4. First sew your star shape, as in 3, and then build out from each arm, as in 1.

5. Running satin stitch blobs. Holding your hoop very firmly, and running the machine fast and continuously, sew a blob and then jog along as soon as the blob is finished, sewing another close by. This can be done in any direction, and is a good filling stitch. The project on pages 62/64 uses this technique.

5

CHAPTER FOUR
Filling Stitches and Needlelace

This delightful embroidery technique is based on machine darning. It goes under a variety of names, cutwork with lace fillings, holework, even air-stitching, all sound far more interesting than darning!

- Unless you have had lessons already, or have worked through the book until now, please don't be tempted just to have a go. At least read Chapters 1 and 2, but all the techniques included will be easier to follow if you first work your way through the book, acquiring skills as you do so.

FILLING STITCHES

The usual set-up
Set up your machine (see page 18), put the fabric in the hoop, (see page 16) and make sure you are sitting comfortably, (see page 17). Stitch length 0, stitch width 0, tension: top normal to loose. Threads: 50 embroidery cotton if possible. If not, whatever you have to hand and contrasting colours to start with.

Preparing the hole
Draw a circle on your fabric, (use a 2cm, 1in button or something similar if necessary), slide the hoop under the needle and remember Four Important Things from page 24.

- Be careful of your fingers, and keep them away from the needle area.

Sew two rows of straight stitching round the circle. Remove the hoop from the machine. Cut the fabric out from inside the stitching with small, sharp-ended scissors, while the fabric is in the hoop.

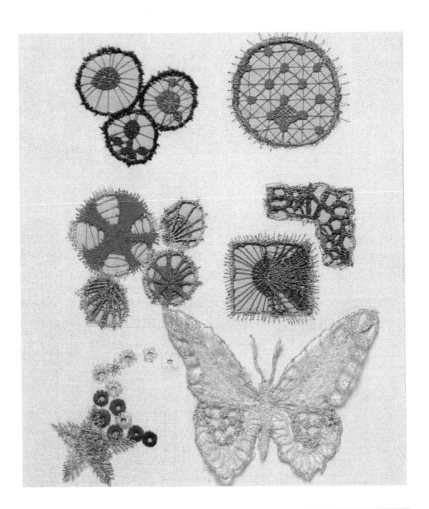

SEWING ON AIR

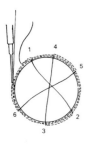

Lower your presser bar lever. Lower your needle on the fabric side of the stitching, and firm in the thread. Sew off across the hole to the other side, to position 2 (opposite), as if you were sewing on fabric, smoothly, so that the sewn thread stays under tension. It might feel a little strange but don't be tentative. If your aim is bad, mark the positions the first few times. Sew round the fabric close to the stitching to 3. Sew off across again to 4, and so on, making a nice cross-web of lines.

Sew to the centre of your cross-web and start sewing round and round like a tight spider's web. When you have achieved a good spiral, run out to the edge and finish off, by firming the thread.

Now you have the basics of filling holes.

This time try a square and fill it up like this.

Remember, don't be tentative with this technique, and keep

your threads smoothly twisted and under tension. If at any time you don't like what you have done, simply cut out the web and start again on the same hole.

Copy the motifs in the colour plate for examples. Do several holes until you become accustomed to sewing patterns. Change and mix colours and thread sizes—experiment and try oversewing several webs with a zigzag stitch to make a thicker web.

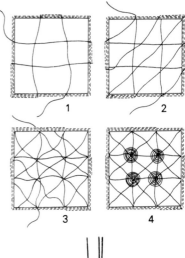

More complicated shapes
Uneven sides must always be thoroughly anchored across the hole before starting, even if that anchor line is cut away later on.

Finishes
To finish off your filled hole, the rough edges must be sewn in. One way this can be done is by careful zigzag or satin stitch oversewing, if it needs to be very neat. There are various finishes illustrated in the colour picture. Only finish small distances at a time, end with your needle in the fabric side of the stitching and then turn the hoop anti-clockwise.

Occasionally you will find some machines don't like darning in one particular direction. You just have to get used to not sewing in that direction. Don't be worried by the pings and pulls whilst you are sewing, they are perfectly normal.

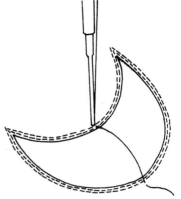

A variation
Small metal lampshade rings, or bent wire, can be filled in this way, but step over the metal edge by turning the flywheel by hand, thus saving yourself from getting through large numbers of broken needles. Tie your threads to start and finish. Stronger threads are probably better if the rings are to be handled.

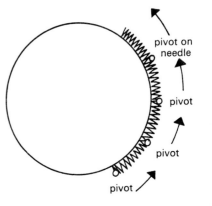

NEEDLELACE

Cold water soluble fabric
In the last couple of years a really exciting new fabric has come on the market. It looks like colourless plastic, and can be sewn on with the machine like any other fabric, but when sprayed or otherwise doused with water, it disappears.

This means that you can sew lacy motifs without cutting

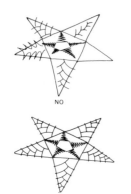

NO

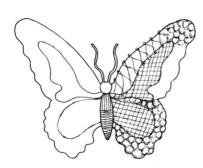

YES

holes in fabric and filling them. The only thing that *must* be remembered is that no single thread should be left unsupported.

When stretching the fabric in the hoop, it must be treated with respect but it can be tightened enough to sew on. You can use straight sewing or zigzag/satin stitch, but if you are going to do heavy satin stitch, it must be the last thing you do, as it can split the fabric.

For stockists and specialist books, see lists on page 91.

- Be careful what you use when drawing your design onto this fabric. The colour may run into your thread if you use the wrong thing. Try drawing the pattern on a piece of paper and pinning it under the fabric, then sewing round the main outlines in the appropriate threads, but remove the paper before sewing any more detailed pattern.

Eyelet holes
If your machine has eyelet hole attachments, they can be used as good additional techniques, especially when combined with built-in stitches, like the blind hemmer or serpentine stitch. The technique is shown on the bird's eye on page 5.

CHAPTER FIVE
Altered Tension Stitches

Most of our machining lives are spent trying to keep the top and bobbin tensions suitably balanced for making dresses or curtains. The following stitches, of which Whip Stitch is my favourite, need the top tension to be tightened on purpose.

- As I have already mentioned, unless you have already had some embroidery lessons on your machine, please at least read through Chapters 1 and 2 to avoid unnecessary difficulty. Preferably, use the book in the way that it has been written, for building on the simplest techniques, and working through to more difficult ones.

TIGHTENING THE TOP THREAD TENSION

If you have been following this book through till now, you may have loosened your top tension. If you have succeeded in getting this far and not altered it in any way, now you must check with your machine handbook, (if you don't already know) and find how to tighten it. Many machines have a numbered tension disc, the Bernina has only a tiny + or − sign. You might well assume that everybody knows how to alter their top tension, but you'd be surprised! I have known students who have been using their machines for dressmaking for years, but when asked to loosen the top tension a trifle, look amazed and tell me they have no idea how to do it!

- When embarking on a stitch that needs the top thread tension tightened, (as we do here) tighten it just a little, and if the stitch doesn't seem to work, tighten it a bit more. The Elna, for instance, can immediately go to 7 or 8, but the Frister Rossman will probably need to go only a little above normal.

When you have found the right tension, make a note of it.

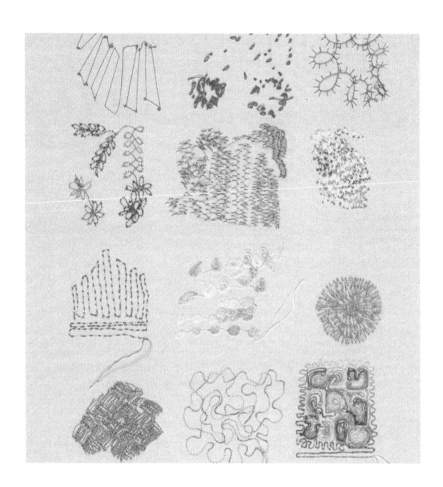

WHIP STITCH

For this you will need ordinary 40 sewing thread, and 50 machine embroidery thread if you have it.

The usual set-up
Set up your machine (see page 18), put the fabric in the hoop (see page 16) and make sure you are sitting comfortably, (see page 17). Stitch length 0, stitch width 0, tensions: top—tightened. Threads: top—ordinary 40 sewing thread, bobbin—50 machine embroidery thread, if possible Contrasting colours, and variegated thread in the bobbin if you have them.

Why 'whip' stitch?
The stitch is formed by the tightened upper tension pulling

the bobbin thread right through to the top of the fabric and whipping it round the thicker top thread. The top thread is also pulled back up and lies neatly along the top of the fabric.

Now begin

- ● **Watch your fingers!**

Run through Four Important Things on page 24. Tighten your top tension a little. When you start to sew run the machine fast, and move the hoop steadily but slowly.

The idea is to cover the top thread completely with the lower thread, so that none of the upper thread shows through. It should be easy to see, if you have contrasting threads.

If your top thread is still being pulled down by the bobbin thread, tighten the tension a little more, until it lies along the top of the fabric. Once you have the knack of it, practice for a while, and then try and follow a few small patterns, which make good filling stitches. Look at the colour plate for examples, and the following variations.

Variations

When you can cover the thicker upper thread fairly evenly with the fine lower thread, try the variations which are on the colour plate opposite.

1. Move the machine on short runs back and forth, next to each other, so that the contrasting upper thread shows through in the centre of the run, and the lower thread builds up at the ends of the runs. This can be done in blocks, or circles, or any direction you wish.

2. As you start to sew, jog the hoop forward a fraction, then hold still for a fraction, jog forward, hold still, and you should build up blobs of lower thread at close intervals along the top thread. I have done lovely raggedy breasted birds using this variation, with the upper thread matching the fabric so that it hardly shows and leaving the coloured bobbin thread to be seen.

3. Now experiment with zigzag stitch, both with mixed thicknesses of threads or similar threads, and see what effects you can get with that.

   Projects on pages 65, 66, 78 and 83 use these techniques.

FEATHER STITCH

- If you don't know how to alter your bobbin tension and get it back to normal, **do not try this stitch.**

It is not my intention in this book to discuss altering your bobbin tension, and the techniques available when you do this. However, if you do know how to alter your bobbin tension and get it back to normal again, (you may have an Elna machine, which has a numbered screw control and is easy to alter and get back to normal again) then read and try this stitch.

Feather stitch is an extension of whip stitch, where the bobbin tension is loosened and the top tension is tightened. Prepare everything as for whip stitch, and when you start, sew in circles and swirls and the lower thread will be pulled into long spikey stitches by the tight top thread. If you sew slowly in ever decreasing circles, you end up with a fluffy looking flower like mimosa or wattle. The slower you sew, the longer the spikey thread will be. Remember to firm in the thread to start and finish.

Then experiment with zigzag stitch, and different threads, experiment with different tensions, and get a grading of effects between whip stitch and feather stitch (see colour plate on page 36).

LONG LEGGED STITCH

This is a simple and obvious stitch when you think about it, with a surprising number of uses. It is included here because the tensions are altered, but in this case by lowering and raising the presser bar lever, and altering the tension on the top thread in this way. See colour plate, page 40.

The set-up
Set up your machine (see page 18), put the fabric in the hoop (see page 16) and make sure you are sitting comfortably (see page 17). Stitch length 0, stitch width 0—4 (your choice), tensions: top—normal to loose. Threads: same top and bobbin

How to do it
- Watch out for your fingers!

Follow the Four Important Things (see page 24) then firm in your thread with a few stitches.

Lift the needle to its highest point by turning the flywheel towards you. Raise the presser bar lever. Move the hoop to where the needle is to be inserted, and then a tiny bit further. **Note**: By moving that tiny bit further than the actual position required, and then putting the needle where it should go, gives the threads a little play and so the material doesn't pull.

Insert the needle in its proper place by turning the flywheel towards you by hand. Lower the presser bar lever. Firm in the stitch and continue as wished. This technique is used in 'Atom', on page 29.

CHAPTER SIX

Thicker Threads and Yarns

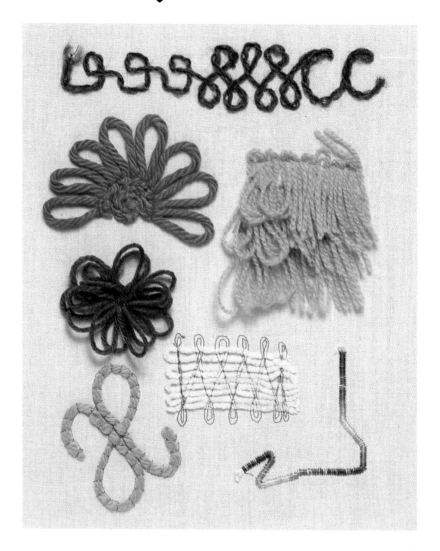

For creative work, it adds interest to use thicker threads and yarns, which will not go through the needle. Here are two ways of working with them.

- Again, if you have not already read through Chapters 1 and 2 it would be advisable for you to do so, unless you have already had lessons in machine embroidery.

HOW TO APPLY THICKER THREADS AND YARNS

The usual set-up

Set up your machine (see page 18), put the fabric in the hoop (see page 16) and make sure you are sitting comfortably, (see page 17). Stitch length 0, stitch width 0, tensions: top—normal. Threads: Top and bobbin: as fine as possible, thick knitting yarn, to apply.

Colours will need to match if possible, but it doesn't matter while you are learning.

How to go about it

Remember Four Important Things in Chapter 3 on page 24.

Use both hands equally for this technique. At first you might feel a little awkward but after one or two hilarious tries you will soon get the knack.

- You will need to use your fingers close up to the needle, so please **be careful**.

Draw a simple pattern on your fabric or, if you feel happier, sew freely.

Firm in your thread. Take your thick knitting yarn, and lower the needle into it by moving the flywheel towards you.

Guiding the hoop with one hand, and the wool with the other, lay the wool on your pattern line, and sew along the wool with small stitches to make them disappear into the work. Change hands as necessary.

- ●● Put your foot on the foot pedal with great caution and use it with control, you don't want sudden spurts of speed with your fingers so vulnerable.

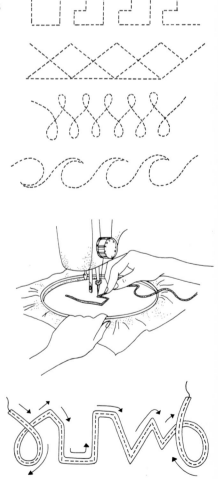

To turn a corner, there is no need to turn your hoop round, just move it sideways and away from you.

However, you may prefer, when sewing spirals, to turn the hoop, making it easier to control the wool.

When you have the knack of sewing your yarn down, try a few experiments. Twist two or three different colours or types together; pull on one ply of the yarn, and push the rest up to make a nice raised or knobbly yarn before sewing it down, tie knots in it or sew loops of unravelled yarn.

If you find it difficult to follow your pattern line, pin your yarn at strategic points, but remove the pins as you come to them—don't sew over them.

Look at the colour plate for examples and the following variations and see how the technique was used in the project on page 67/68.

VARIATIONS

Flat loops
Instead of sewing continuously through your yarn or thread, lay it in a loop flat on the fabric and only sew across the narrow end. The loops can also be sewn in series.

If you cut the loop ends, you are left with a loose piled effect, easier to sew than separate little bits of yarn.

Raised loops

Instead of laying the narrow ends of your loop side by side as in the flat loop, cross them over and make the loop stand up. Sew another opposite the first, and then another between those and so on, until you have built up a little rosette of loops that sit right off the fabric.

Oversewn yarn
Lay the threads or yarns side by side and pin or hold sew them at the edges to keep them together. Then oversew them with a free pattern, incorporating yarns and stitching into the design.

See the colour plate, page 40.

COUCHING THICKER THREADS AND YARNS

There are two methods for couching—heavy covering and light covering. Follow the usual set-up, on page 41. Threads: top and bobbin: whichever is applicable, thick yarn or thread. The colour of your threads depends very much on whether you want them to show or disappear. For practice it doesn't matter.

- You will need to use your fingers very close to the needle, so please **be careful**. Watch the pressure on your foot pedal, and don't make a sudden surge of movement.

Heavy covering

In this variation, the colour of the machine threads is important, as they completely cover the thick thread. Choose a thick, firm thread, like a heavy crochet cotton, or even a fine twine, for practice. Firm in your machine thread. Choose a stitch width that will go just neatly over the thick thread.

Lay your thick thread under your needle, and turn the flywheel by hand a couple of stitches to oversew the end and keep it stable. Holding the hoop with one hand, and guiding the thread with the other, oversew the thick thread carefully with a smooth, close satin stitch.

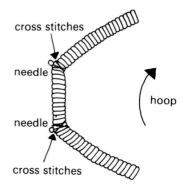

- Make sure that on corners and sharp bends, you end with the needle in the fabric on the outside of a bend, and the inside of a sharp corner, before turning the hoop.

You may need a less smooth appearance to your work, in which case, run a fine zigzag stitch back and forth to cover the thick thread.

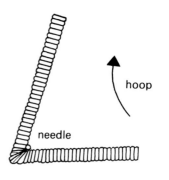

- If you pin the thick thread into place, stop at each pin and remove it, don't be tempted to sew over it.

Light covering

In this variation, the colour of the thicker thread or yarn is more important, as it will be seen, so match your machine threads if necessary.

If your machine has a built-in, blind hemming stitch this can be used, or you may have an even more suitable built-in stitch—Elnadisc 150, for instance. All is not lost however, if you don't have any built-in stitches. If just means that you have to think for yourself instead of having your machine do it for you!

- Your fingers are very close to the needle, so **take care**.

Firm in your machine thread. Set your machine for blind hemming or for your chosen stitch. (If you have neither, your instruction follow.) Adjust the stitch width to suit the thickness of your chosen thread or yarn. (These built-in stitches are sewn freely on the hoop fabric, without the foot.) Lay your thick thread by the needle and, holding the hoop in one hand and the thick thread in the other, slowly start to sew, running the straight stitch very close to the edge of the thicker yarn.

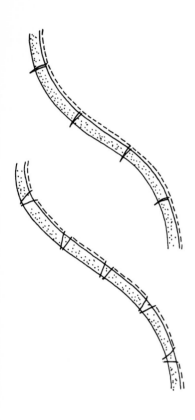

- Don't start to sew with a sudden surge of speed, use a careful pressure on the foot pedal.

When the stitch side-steps for the single zigzag stitch, either stop moving the hoop and let the zigzag stitch step back into the hole it started from, and so only appear to have a one stitch oversew; or carry on moving the hoop and so get an open zigzag stitch.

If you have no built-in stitches:
The alternative to having a built-in stitch is that you yourself simply move the hoop to make the side stitch. Sew alongside the thick thread and when appropriate move the hoop sideways to sew a stitch over the thick thread and then back again. If your machine will not sew extremely slowly to enable you to control the stitch then stop and turn the flywheel by hand. This is not nearly as laborious as you think, and works very well.

- Exert gentle pressure on the foot pedal to avoid a sudden rush of speed.

CHAPTER SEVEN
An Introduction to Appliqué

Appliqué is sewing—or applying—one piece of fabric in the form of a pattern, onto a different, backing fabric, so you will need both appliqué fabric and the backing fabric.

HOW CAN IT BE USED?

Appliqué can be a sewing technique used as an end in itself; or it can be used along with the embroidery techniques learned from this book. A piece of appliquéd fabric can replace an area of heavy stitching, with some more delicate, descriptive embroidery sewn on top to give a better effect; the appliquéd fabric can be sewn on with free machine embroidery; or both appliqué and creative embroidery can be used together in an abstract way; and so on. The choice is very wide.

Fabrics
In this book I assume that both appliqué and backing fabrics will be of similar type and weight. You can, however, use any fabric from nets and fine fabrics through to cottons and leather.

How to use this chapter
Read the chapter through first, and then decide which method suits your design best. I have divided the techniques of appliqué into four stages, one leading to the next, so that it will be necessary to use each stage to make a complete appliqué technique.

STAGE 1: TO HOOP OR NOT TO HOOP

● *In the hoop* Fabrics can be applied by embroidering creatively without a foot, *or* you can use presser foot and feed dogs for very controlled work (see page 16).
● *Out of the hoop* You can apply fabrics with presser foot and feed dogs, *or* sew freely and creatively with the darning foot and no feed dogs.

When using the darning foot, either the fabric must be very firm (like jean or denim), or have enough layers to be very firm. If not, it will need to be backed, by paper perhaps. This is because the fabric itself must be held in both hands and pressed firmly against the machine bed, so that control will be as free as if the fabric were stretched in a hoop.

STAGE 2: PUTTING A DESIGN ONTO THE APPLIQUÉ FABRIC

1. *Bondaweb*—this a commercial, adhesive web, attached to

paper. Draw your design in reverse on the paper, cut it out a bit bigger than the actual design, leaving a small margin round the outside, (the margin makes it easier to cut out the design accurately). Iron it on to the wrong side of the appliqué fabric, then cut out the actual design.

2. *Use a pattern* to cut out the design from the appliqué fabric.

3. *Draw or trace* your design onto the appliqué fabric, (if you don't know how to do this see page 54).

4. *Sew through paper* It is possible to sew directly through a design outlined on paper, or to sew round the edge of a paper shape. But you will be restricted as to the size of your design if you are going to use a hoop, as you can't stretch paper in a hoop.

STAGE 3: PREPARING FABRIC FOR APPLIQUÉ

1. *Bondaweb*—remove the backing paper from your cut out shape, and iron it onto the backing fabric, following the instructions on the packet.

2. *Cut out appliqué shapes*—either **tack** the cut out appliqué fabric design onto the backing, by firming it in places with cross-tacking, and then, smoothing the fabric carefully as you go, tack round just inside the edge of the design. Or **pin** at right angles to the pattern line. Put the first pin at the top, the next at the bottom, then one at the two sides, smoothing the fabric carefully as you go. Then halve each of those spaces with a pin, and halve each again, until you have a pin every 1cm, $\frac{1}{2}$in or so.

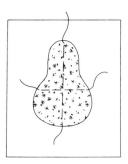

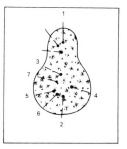

● Be careful of the pins if the applied shape is larger than the hoop.

● It is quite all right to hoop up across the design.

3. *Large piece of appliqué fabric*—when both appliqué and backing are large enough to go into a hoop together. Lay the backing fabric as it will eventually be positioned, then lay the appliqué fabric over it, trying if possible to match the grains. This ensures that both fabrics sit comfortably with each other.

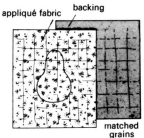

appliqué fabric   backing

matched grains

Tack or pin through the fabrics to hold them firmly and smoothly together. Then tack round the drawn or traced design just inside its edge, or pin it, as in 2 overleaf. *Or* tack or pin the paper pattern or paper cut out onto the appliqué fabric, also as in 2 overleaf. (If the pattern is small enough it is even possible to pin it on when the fabric is already in the hoop.) Then hoop-up.

STAGE 4: SEWING TECHNIQUES

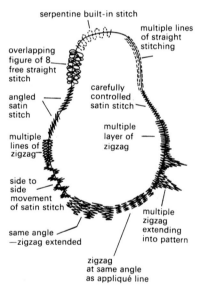

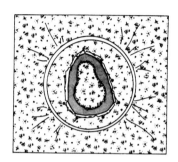

serpentine built-in stitch

multiple lines of straight stitching

overlapping figure of 8 free straight stitch

carefully controlled satin stitch

angled satin stitch

multiple layer of zigzag

multiple lines of zigzag

side to side movement of satin stitch

multiple zigzag extending into pattern

same angle —zigzag extended

zigzag at same angle as appliqué line

Initial sewing

Straight stitching—when you have both fabrics in the hoop as in 3 overleaf, sew round the design outline with straight stitching and remove the hoop from the machine. Then with the fabrics still in the hoop, carefully cut round the outside of the appliqué design as close to the stitching as possible.

With the fabric still in the hoop, pin the remaining fabric back out of the way—you may need a little snip here and there to do so. Don't try taking it out of the hoop to get rid of the surplus material, you'll never get it sitting back exactly as it was before.

Sewing through paper—if the appliqué pattern is going to be sewn initially directly through a paper design, it is not difficult, with care, to tear away the paper as if it had a perforated line. But don't just give it the old heave-ho, you may rip the stitches! Once the outline is sewn, remove all the paper pattern.

- Remove all pins as you come to them—don't sew over them.

Applying a cut out shape—you may find it easier initially to sew round the outside of your shape with a narrow zigzag to hold it firm until you are used to applying your pieces. Of course, if you intend to use a straight sewing technique then don't use the zigzag!

Final stitching

Free stitching—the usual set-up. Without the hoop, work with the embroidery foot on; in the hoop, set up the machine as indicated on page 18. (The fabric will be in the hoop already.) Then, make sure you are sitting comfortably (see page 17). Stitch length 0, stitch width as needed, tensions: top—normal to loose, threads: your choice top and bobbin. Remember the Four Important Things. Now oversew the edge of your appliqué; the picture and instructions will give you some idea of what to do. It is a good idea to do several practice pieces first, and you will then find you are inventing ideas of your own.

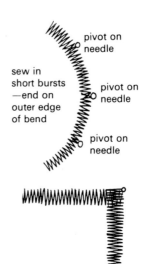

- If you want to have a very smooth satin stitch round your appliqué, then use the presser foot and feed dogs—even in the hoop. The projects on pages 69 and 86 use this technique.

When sewing a curve in your design, sew in short runs, ending with the needle on the outside of the curve in the fabric, and pivot on the needle, thus keeping your sewing line. See the colour plate on page 45.

When sewing a corner, always pivot on your needle. Sew right into the corner at your chosen stitch width, pivot on the needle, and continue sewing.

HINTS

If your appliqué fabric is puckered, it might help to snip the backing fabric behind the appliqué to release tension, if it is appropriate for the particular item being sewn.

If the appliqué on a garment has ended up thick and bulky, cut away the backing as in *Insertion* below (again, if appropriate).

If you are doing a piece of work with several separate pieces of appliqué, work out your plan of campaign first, so that all the pieces are sewn on in the right order!

INSERTION

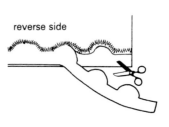

Insertion is one step on from appliqué, and a good example are the lace inserts in underwear—around the bottom of slips and across the tops of petticoats. It is an excellent technique for making clothes and house linen look more attractive and special.

Use any of the appliqué methods from this chapter, except the Bondaweb, to apply your lace motif, or piece of fabric. When it has been firmly oversewn onto the right side of your fabric, turn the work over and very carefully cut away the backing fabric, inside the stitching, with small sharp scissors, making sure that you don't cut yourself a neat hole by snipping through the front layer too!

The projects on page 71 use this technique.

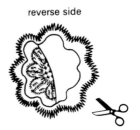

CHAPTER EIGHT
Looking at Colour and Design

- Always try out your ideas on a practice hoop, it can save hours of miserable unpicking! Try out even the wildest idea, nobody is going to see it if it doesn't work.

LIGHT AND COLOUR IN YOUR USE OF THREADS

Look back at the work you have done while following the earlier chapters of this book and look at the colour photographs; see what effect different colours and textures have on each other.

Stitch lengths
Notice how short stitches disappear into the fabric and how the light picks up and accentuates long stitches—especially in your early, less controlled work, where the odd long stitch sticks out!

Bobbin threads
See how a lighter bobbin thread gives a translucent look as it is pulled up at the end of runs of stitching; see how a darker bobbin colour adds depth to your work.

Nothing is flat colour
Light and shade affect everything. Try and see how best to use your coloured threads in the bobbin or on the top, to achieve the effect you want.

Vary thread thickness
Use a different sized thread in a similar colour, side by side, to bring your work forward, and give it depth.

Colour contrast
If you machine round a lighter coloured piece of work with a darker stitch, it pushes the lighter work forward.

Blending

It is easy in creative embroidery on the machine to run one colour into another by oversewing at the edge of each colour block. A good effect can be created by shading in the darker and lighter colours at the sides of an object, to give it shape.

Fur and feathers

Look into animal fur and see how shadows give it depth, or in dark fur, notice highlights of reflected light. When sewing a white bird I used more greys than white, using white only for well lit areas and highlights.

Animal textures

Find the right texture for the coat of an animal: short straight stitch movements look shaggy; closely oversewn wide zigzags pick up the light and create a smooth shiny fur effect. Close spirals of whip stitch for sheep, and angled, even satin stitch for feathers.

● Always keep all of your practice pieces until you are sure that you won't want them again. So often you can use them to spot exactly the technique, or use a stitch that you are looking for. If you feel inclined, note on the practice pieces the details of the textures you particularly like.

DESIGN

Sources of inspiration

Some people are overflowing with original ideas but don't worry if you are not one of these, start being a magpie. Collect picture postcards, photographs, greetings cards, pictures from calendars, pictures from magazines, designs from childrens' painting books, pictures of paintings, or of other peoples' embroidery to give you ideas. Scour your local libraries for books on design, or books on the subject you are wanting to design. The most novel ideas must come from somewhere.

Copy

Unless you are going to use the idea commercially, (in which case you must check the copyright), quite blatantly copy other people's work. A great deal can be learnt as an apprentice by copying as it can form a fertile grounding from which your own ideas will grow. Try copying Joy Clucas's work on pages 5 and 29.

Embroidery of Corinne's Bird

How to approach it—hints

When designing for creative embroidery on the sewing machine, don't be tempted to include too much drawn detail in advance. It isn't like hand embroidery and excellent ideas will develop as you go along.

Draw an outline, and give yourself an idea of the main areas of colour and texture, and perhaps an indication of the stitching direction. Look at the design of Corinne's Bird above. Choose possible textures, thread types and the colours you want to use.

- Always do a test run on a practice hoop. If you can't quite make up your mind which stitch or texture to use, look back over practice pieces you have done and try to find what you are looking for, and experiment with it until you get it right.

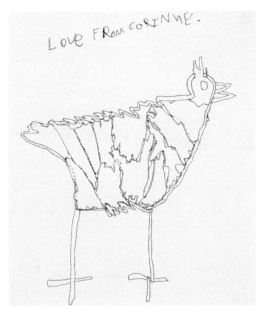

Left. Original drawing

Right. Design of embroidery

Look carefully at your design and see where to start and in what order you will have to do things. If you are working a furry animal, you have to start sewing at the tail end in order to imitate the lie of the fur. A furry face will only have the right character if you follow the way the fur lies. If you want to do a bird, build it up from its head, breast and feet to wings; the way the feathers lie on its head will also give the bird its particular character.

The background of a picture must be worked before its foreground and main features. For example, if you look at the original of Corinne's Bird, you'll see that she drew the outline first. The eye was put in over the grey of the head. Some colours were drawn over the top of different colours, while others were used more heavily to give varying intensities of the same colour. The colouring strokes also vary; some are wide while some are narrow and sharply drawn. The result is a mass of colour and texture—perfect to embroider.

This is a nice idea for grannies and mums to copy, when they are presented with a particularly good piece of colouring, but often, alas, on odd bits of scrap paper.

LARGER OR SMALLER

If, for instance, you are copying a design from a postcard, trace it onto clean paper, only putting in the main areas of

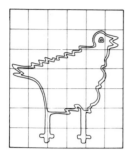

detail. Draw a grid over it, as in the illustration.

Choose the new size for your design, and draw the measurements onto a new sheet of paper. Inside this space draw another grid composed of the same number of squares as drawn on the original tracing. Copy the original design square by square, thus making a bigger version. You will not find this at all difficult, just take your time.

TRANSFERRING THE DESIGN

Before you start, make sure that your outline is clear and dark, perhaps use a fine felt-tipped pen.

One of the easiest ways to transfer the design onto fabric is to stick the drawing onto a window with masking tape, then over the top of that, in the appropriate position, stick your fabric. Using firm, clean lines you can then simply trace the design onto the fabric with a very hard pencil. You can get a lot of graphite on the fabric without it showing too much, even unused lines don't show unless you know just where they are.

● Should you want to do this at night, then reverse things and stick everything on the outside of the window, assuming your windows are nice and clean!

Sometimes it is possible to see a dark outline clearly enough through the fabric to trace without using the window. Robbie Fanning in her book (see bibliography) suggests using the television screen on an empty channel.

It is worth trying an air erasable marking pen which has recently been brought onto the market. The ink in the pen takes from a few hours to a few days, depending upon the humidity of the air, to disappear.

● For dark fabrics use a tailor's chalk pencil.

If you are going to embroider a garment which you are making, it is always easier to embroider on the flat uncut piece of fabric first. Draw the appropriate garment piece onto the fabric, and embroider just where you want it. This is *much* easier than trying to fit a finished garment into a hoop, or trying to get it right without a hoop, but using the darning foot.

CHAPTER NINE
Stretching and Mounting

When you have completed a piece of work which is to hang on a wall or in some way needs to stand, rather than lie as in a table cloth, it may be puckered—how much depends on the amount of work done. To straighten it out again, it can be stretched over either firm card, if there is no need for great tension, or board or ply wood if it is going to be really under tension. You can then frame it, have it framed, or in some way mount it.

STRETCHING THE EMBROIDERY

Work out the finished size of your embroidery, if you are having a coloured board border, take that into consideration before cutting your fabric.

Cut, or have cut, a piece of hardboard to size. Thick card will do provided the work does not have to be under a lot of stretched tension, as it will bend. Smooth off the edges with sandpaper so that the fabric will slip round easily. Trim the embroidery to an overlap of 4cm, 1½in—8cm, 3in at each edge, depending on the size of your work. Sew bias binding along each edge, (polycotton is best but not essential), using serpentine stitch. Strengthen the outer edge by sewing a couple of rows of closely sewn stitching.

- The serpentine stitch will ease with the fabric when it is being stretched. The strengthening rows prevent the polycotton from splitting through.

If the work is to be under very great tension, sew a double layer of bias binding round the work, face to face, sewing the rows of closely sewn stitching through both layers of edge, to join them together.

Carefully iron or press around the edge of the work on the reverse. The embroidery itself should only be ironed gently on

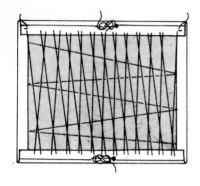

the reverse if absolutely necessary and never steam pressed, or it will flatten and ruin your work. If it will not come straight, put it back in its hoop and iron it stretched. Allow to cool for a short while before removing. Traditional methods of pressing and stretching may, of course, be used.

Lay the work face down on a clean table and table cloth with the board on top, in place.

Bring the sides over and lace from both ends to off centre, firmly, with fine carpet thread or twine. Check that the board is correctly placed, then fix temporarily by winding the ends round a pin. Keep tightening and stretching until all the creases are gone (pull the fabric manually in the other directions to check), then sew off or knot off.

Bring the other side over, lacing in the same way, until the work is unwrinkled (or as nearly as possible) and smoothly stretched, and then sew off or knot off, permanently. Tidy away the fabric at the corners as you wish, either by tucking it in or sewing it down. If you trim the fabric, think into the future, as sometime your work may need to be washed or remounted.

Cover the lacings as you wish. You can iron on a narrow strip of Bondaweb round the edge of the fabric for the backing, and actually iron it on to the back of the picture. This does work very well, and is the method I use. Or you can sew it by hand. If it is to be professionally mounted, then the framer will back it.

Finally Make a note of the reference number of your machine, and when putting it away, always store the foot pedal in a separate place from the machine, so that should the machine be stolen the thief or whoever buys it from him, will have to seek a new foot pedal, and the machine will have a better chance of being traced and recovered.

PROJECTS

Once you have a technique at your fingertips, have a go at an appropriate project to give you practice. These designs are not just meant to be pictures. Practice first, and then use them on a tea cosy, a dress, a table cloth or whatever. If you feel you can improve on any project then do so.

If you are not going to stretch the embroidery, then watch your tensions.

Don't panic if my idea of 'easy' turns out to be your idea of difficult, none of us works in the same way. If you haven't done any embroidery on the machine for a while, practice to get your fingers working.

The projects on pages 57–61 are easy, and you should have a lot of fun with these straight away. On pages 62–71 the projects are easy to medium. By pages 74–79 they are more daring. (Bella on page 74 is much simpler than it looks.)

Pages 82–86 are challenges. They either involve mixed techniques or need very fine sewing.

GREETINGS CARDS

Greetings cards

Reeds and Duck

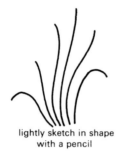

sew round all the lines
at least twice

bull rush head

lightly sketch in shape
with a pencil

leaf filling

sew up and down
for leaves

Technique from Chapter 3.
Scale of fabric pieces 12cm, 5in × 8cm, 3in. For information on pattern transfer and enlargement see Chapter 8.

The sheep are stuck on a proper card mount. Sewn on sheeting using 50 machine embroidery thread, put your stitch width at 0. You will need a very hard 4H pencil.

the hedge is a
squiggly line,
filled in with
more squiggles

Sheep

a

draw a box
lightly in pencil

b

sew round the
outside and fill with
curls

c

all head, ears, eye and
legs all in one run (start
with right ear, left ear,
face, eye, legs)
sew round the outside
again and over the dark
line under the body
joining the legs

Instructions
These cards are surprisingly easy—send to friends or relations for any occasion.

- When sewing the designs, your stitches may not fit exactly over the pencil outline, so draw very lightly.
- Keep your stitches fairly long in case you have to unpick them! If you do, use a seam ripper and unpick from the back of your work.
- A little waywardness adds life so don't worry at all about wobbly lines unless they are real wobblies—when you just unpick and re-sew them.

Hints for your own design
If you don't feel like sewing ducks and sheep use one of the line patterns as a border used in the little Tooth Fairy Pillows on page 60. If you don't like the duck in the picture, make the bottom of the picture at the bottom of the reeds, and take the picture in a small distance from the left hand side. Try out your own ideas.

TOOTH FAIRY PILLOWS

Technique from Chapter 3, illustration on page 60.
For pattern transfer and enlargement see Chapter 8.

This design

All sewn on sheeting using 50 machine embroidery thread, Madeira Gold metallic and ordinary sewing cotton for construction. Use polyester wadding scraps for stuffing and gold fabric scrap for the pocket.

Instructions

Use the same thread top and bottom with the top tension loose for embroidery and normal for construction. With the stitch width at 0, keep the stitches a good length as you may need to unpick some work! Please practice on a spare hoop first. Sew the pockets on with the fabric still in the hoop.

- Write the words in pencil on paper to get the feel of actually forming the letters first.
- Always draw a very faint guide line when sewing words.
- Use 'Mary's tooth' pattern for longer names 1.
- Sew the rainbow first starting from red, then put on the pocket and sew the words 2. The pocket may go on in slightly the wrong position which will put the words out of balance if you sew them first.
- Sew the engine first, then embroider the cushion fabric, then the pocket has to be sewn on, and carefully aligned, then the railway line 3.

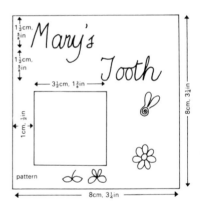

1

When sewing the train, it can be done all in one continuous line (except for the little round window). The carriages can also be sewn all in one go—work that out before you start.

Your lines may well wiggle a little, but don't worry, straight lines come with practice. You will be oversewing the lines twice, and the second time round hides a multitude of sins! Any really wobbly lines can be picked out and re-sewn.

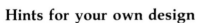

Hints for your own design

These are only ideas for you to try, or to get your mind working. Perhaps your child likes shells, sheep or frogs! Try differently shaped pillows—hearts, triangles, stars, six sided shapes; embroider them with multicoloured hearts, or triangles, stars, or six sided shapes. perhaps put the child's

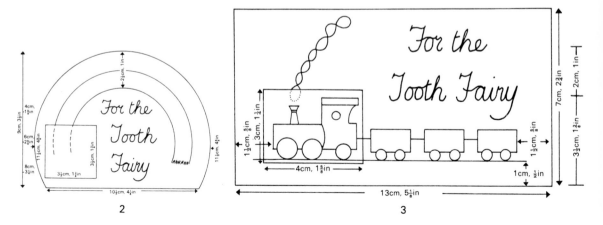

Tooth fairy

name on the back of the cushion. Change the words about, or choose your own. The 3.5cm, 1½in pocket holds most coins.

2

3

JACOBEAN TULIP

A Jacobean Tulip

Taken from an original embroidery in the
Victoria and Albert Museum, London

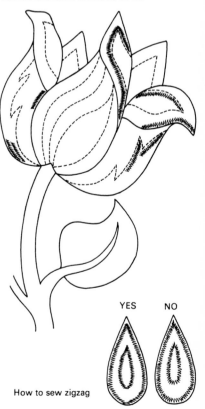

YES   NO

How to sew zigzag

Technique from Chapter 3.
The size of the embroidery measures 16cm, $6\frac{1}{2}$in × 14cm, $5\frac{1}{2}$in.
For information on pattern transfer and enlargement, see
pages 53–54.

This design
Sewn on sheeting. 50 machine embroidery thread.

Instructions
Use the same thread top and bobbin with a loose top tension
and the stitch widths vary. Check colours and tensions on a
practice hoop first. For stretching and mounting see Chapter 9.

- Choose a direction for the zigzag stitch to lie, and keep it
  sewing in the same direction throughout each petal, leaf or
  stem (see illustration right).

- Use the same stitch width over all the flower but slightly larger on the stem and leaf.
- If the edge looks a bit wobbly, outline the edges of leaves, stem or petals with a couple of rows of straight stitching.

Hints for your own design
This can be sewn with a variety of other stitches and techniques from later chapters. There is a set of such patterns by Linda Ormesson, in the bibliography. Look at pictures of real Jacobean embroidery and see what fun they had with colour and stitches.

GOLDEN FISH

All techniques from Chapter 3, illustration on page 64.
Overall scale of embroidery 24cm, $9\frac{1}{2}$in × 18cm, 7in. For pattern transfer and enlargement, see pages 53 and 54.

This design
Sewn on sheeting using Madeira or metallic thread: Gold, silver and colour for eye.

Instructions
Use the same thread top and bobbin with a loose top tension and stitch width 0 to full width. Check all tensions on a practice hoop first. Remove the work from the hoop to check, if it is not to be stretched; to stretch and mount, see page 55.

Golden fish

all marked lines on the fins and tail are contrast lines

body from gill to tail—oversew with wide zigzag stitch over satin blobs

$\frac{3}{4}$ width running satin stitch blobs

full width running satin stitch blobs

all fins and tail —straight stitching

body—outline twice with straight stiching

$\frac{1}{2}$ width running satin stitch blobs

very narrow long stitched zigzag

- Sew satin stitch blobs as indicated, in gold top and bobbin.
- Outline head and body with two rows of straight stitching (thus hiding any irregularities of blobs), and fill in the mouth. Sew the outer ring of the eye, and the gill in straight stitching—all in gold.
- Sew rows of open zigzag over the blobs and up to the gill. Silver top and bobbin. Fill in the rest of the face with very narrow, quite long zigzag, all in silver.
- Outline and sew the fins and tail with fairly close rows of straight stitching, and good length stitches—in silver.

- Sew contrast lines on tail and fins as indicated, straight stitching and good length stitches. Finish tail ends with waivers—gold top and bobbin.
- Now sew pupil of eye in straight stitching as indicated—Effektgarn 5232 top and bobbin or any other suitable thread.

All stitching, including satin stitch, zigzag and straight are sewn with long stitches to catch the light from different angles.

Note: The golden fish is the same basic design as Stripey Cyril.

STRIPEY CYRIL

Techniques from Chapter 3, illustration on page 64.
Overall scale of embroidery 26cm, $10\frac{1}{4}$in by 22cm, $8\frac{1}{2}$in. See pages 53 and 54 for information on pattern transfer and enlargement.

This design
Sewn on sheeting, using 50 machine embroidery thread as follows: black, red and pink top, cream bobbin: Light and dark green top, white bobbin.

Instructions
Use contrasting threads top and bobbin, with a loose top tension. Use a stitch width only just on zigzag, and straight stitching for the eye. Try out the technique on your practice hoop first. If the work needs mounting, see page 55.

- Outline each red and pink area first, and then fill in.
- Fill in the fins and tail, stripe by stripe.
- Sew the eye in straight stitching, outside first, then pupil in black still with white in the bobbin.

Hints for your own design:
Stripey Cyril is the same basic shape as the Golden Fish—it's a fun shape to play with!

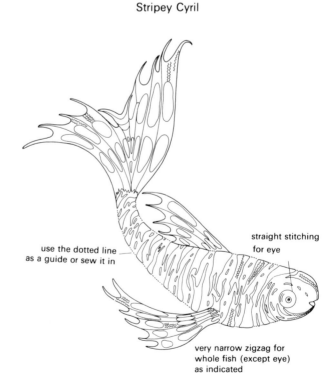

Stripey Cyril

use the dotted line as a guide or sew it in

straight stitching for eye

very narrow zigzag for whole fish (except eye) as indicated

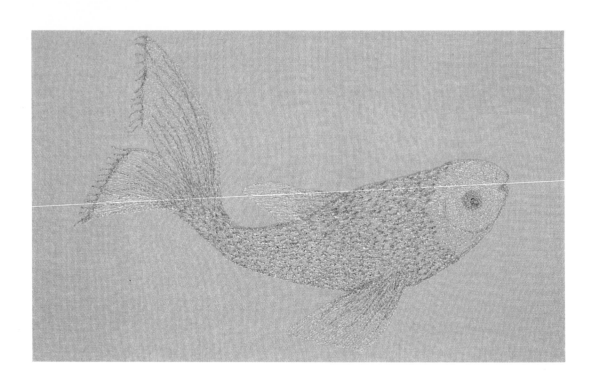

JACOBEAN FANCY

Techniques from Chapters 3 and 5.
Overall size of embroidery 17cm, $6\frac{3}{4}$in $\times$ $15\frac{1}{2}$cm, 6in. For pattern transfer and enlargement see pages 53 and 54.

This design
Sewn on sheeting using 50 machine embroidery thread for petals and veins, ordinary sewing thread and variegated machine embroidery thread for leaf filling and plain coloured machine embroidery thread for edging.

Instructions
Use the same thread top and bobbin for petals and veins, ordinary sewing thread top and machine embroidery cotton bobbin for leaf. Top tensions: for satin stitch and zigzag loose; for whip stitch tight. Stitch width 0–full width. Try out the techniques on a practice hoop first. If the work needs stretching and mounting, see page 55.

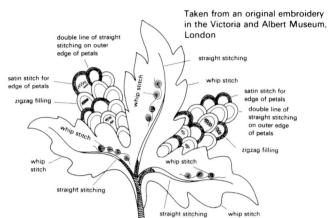

Jacobean Fancy

Taken from an original embroidery in the Victoria and Albert Museum, London

double line of straight stitching on outer edge of petals

straight stitching

whip stitch

satin stitch for edge of petals

zigzag filling

whip stitch

satin stitch for edge of petals

double line of straight stitching on outer edge of petals

zigzag filling

whip stitch

whip stitch

whip stitch

straight stitching

straight stitching

whip stitch

close zigzag filling

- Sew the satin stitch outlines of the petals, then fill each petal with zigzag.
- Outline the petal edges with straight stitching. Use a darker shade if the petal is very pale.
- Sew the leaf vein outline with straight stitching and fill with close zigzag as indicated.
- Outline the leaf in whip stitch.
- Fill in the leaf as indicated, with whip stitch.

Hints for your own design

This shape can be filled with a large variety of techniques and textures from other chapters of this book. Jacobean embroidery is a great source of inspiration, look at books or in museums for ideas. See Linda Ormesson in the bibliography.

LITTLE BLACK LAMB

Technique from Chapter 5, illustration on page 68.

The size of the embroidery is 16cm, $6\frac{1}{2}$in nose to tail. For pattern transfer and enlargement, see pages 53 and 54.

This design

Sewn on sheeting using bobbin thread: body in variegated black and grey, the rest in pale grey, DMC 50 machine embroidery thread—top thread: body in white, face, tail and nearest legs in black, furthest legs elephant grey, hooves, nose, mouth, eye outline, pupil and ear shading pale grey, ordinary sewing thread.

Instructions

Use ordinary sewing thread top, 50 machine embroidery thread bobbin with the top tension normal to looser for ordinary sewing and raised for whip stitch—stitch width 0. Practice all stitching on a practice hoop. To mount the work, see page 55.

- Whip stitch for body.
- Ordinary straight sewing for rest.

Hints for your own design

If you have no variegated thread, use two colours, sew one colour leaving spaces to fill with the other colour, giving a good variegated appearance. If you use light colours, the further away legs and ear shading will have to be darker. The lamb could be a sheep with a longer more shaggy coat, and not necessarily variegated.

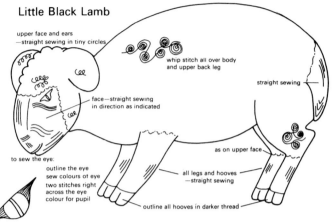

Little Black Lamb

upper face and ears
—straight sewing in tiny circles

whip stitch all over body and upper back leg

straight sewing

face—straight sewing in direction as indicated

as on upper face

to sew the eye:
outline the eye
sew colours of eye
two stitches right
across the eye
colour for pupil

all legs and hooves
—straight sewing

outline all hooves in darker thread

TISSUE BOX COVER

Techniques from Chapter 6, illustration on page 68.
Although the marked grid round the design is 2cm, 1in, to make it fit the average tissue box, the scale of actual work will be on a 3cm, $1\frac{1}{4}$in grid. Check on page 53 for enlarging patterns with grids. If, when you have drawn your 3cm, $1\frac{1}{4}$in grid, you find it difficult to fit the pattern into it, divide the squares of both grids in half and you will have more squares to work with.

This design

Sewn on sheeting using thick knitting wool, candlewick, Madeira, or any similar metallic thread or 50 machine embroidery cotton.

Instructions

Use the same thread top and bobbin with a normal to loose top tension and stitch width 0. A 30cm, 12in hoop will be needed for box side (2). Check the new techniques on a practice hoop first.

- Pull one ply of the wool so that the rest is all pushed up and knobbly.

- With a matching thread, sew through the pushed up wool with straight stitching, as in the illustration for box end,

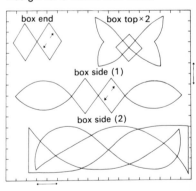

Design for a tissue box cover

box end   box top × 2

box side (1)

box side (2)

Measurement between arrows is 2cm, 1in.

Above. Little Black
 Lamb

Right. Tissue box
 cover.

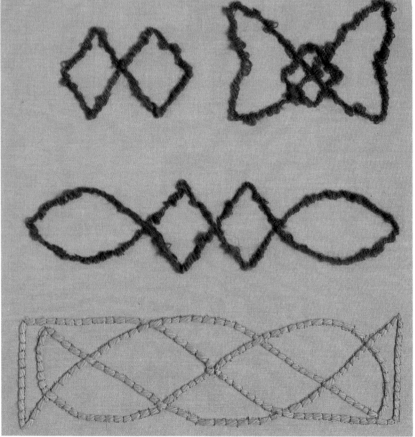

top and side (1). Start and finish where the yarn crosses to hide the join.

- Box side (2) is candlewick, oversewn with Maderia or any similar metallic thread. Straight stitch along one side of the yarn, side-step over the yarn and back by moving the hoop from side to side every so often. This is actually quite quick and easy, and has the advantage of being able to be worked towards you or away from you.

Hints for your own design
The box cover shown is held on by elastic, passing round and just underneath the box to hide the casing. Any form of applied yarn, thread or ribbon can be used for this design. See the book on Celtic design in the bibliography, to inspire new ideas of your own.

OLD LONDON TAXI

Technique from Chapter 7, illustration on page 69.

This design

Sewn on sheeting as backing fabric, with cotton dressmaking fabric and net using 50 machine embroidery cotton. The foot and feed are needed for satin stitch.

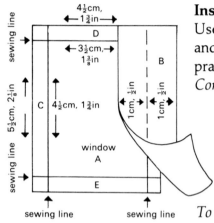

Instructions

Use the same thread top and bobbin with a loose top tension and stitch width at full width. Check your satin stitch on a practice hoop. If the work is to be stretched, see page 55.

Construct 1 as follows:

Window A: size 3.5cm, $1\frac{3}{8}$ × 4.5cm, $1\frac{3}{4}$in plus 0.5cm, $\frac{3}{4}$in seam allowance, in net and fabric.

Frame B,C,D: 5.5cm, $2\frac{1}{8}$in × 2cm, $\frac{3}{4}$in pieces

Panel E: as design, plus 0.5cm, $\frac{1}{4}$in seam allowance on window edge.

To sew:

- Place centre of B face down over sewing line as shown. Sew along line, fold out and press.
- Repeat for C, then D, then E.
- Using the Bondaweb technique, iron 1–5 on to backing fabric in order and place the work into a 23cm, 9in hoop.
- First sew blue satin stitch lines, then door bottom, engine, driver's window from top, back, from the wheel, over the roof, and top of driver's window. All your line ends should then be sewn in. Complete the radiator outline, flowers and door handle.

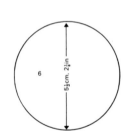

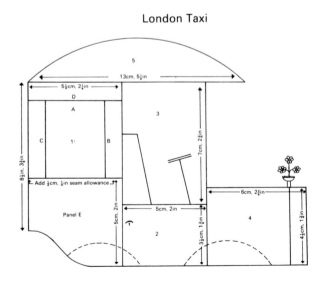

London Taxi

Iron on the wheels, then satin stitch carefully round centimeter by centimeter, (a blind hemmer was used in picture). Add speed swirls if wished.

Complete by sewing round the inner edge of the hoop, using it as a guide.

Hints for your own design

This was originally a cushion. There is netting only in the passenger window as drivers didn't have windows in old London taxis. Use lots of different scraps of fabric, and a good contrast for the satin stitch.

INSERTED MOTIFS ON NET CURTAIN

Techniques from Chapter 7, illustration on page 72.

This design

I used odd bits of lace and net curtaining for these two bathroom curtains. Check the placing of motifs with the curtain *in situ* to see that they look right. Machine embroidery thread was used, but ordinary thread would do as well. Use the insertion technique.

Instructions

Use machine embroidery thread top and bobbin, to suit lace with the top tension normal to loose. Have the stitch width at half full width—use an embroidery foot for the edging. Always experiment on your practice hoop before committing yourself and your fabric.

Curtain 1

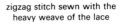

zigzag stitch sewn with the heavy weave of the lace

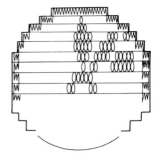

- Pin medallion onto net as on page 47, then place net into hoop with medallion uppermost. Zigzag round medallion edge, keeping the stitch running the same way as the heavy weave of the lace so that it doesn't show, removing each pin as it comes, as in illustration. Finish with a few straight stitches.
- Cut away net from behind the medallion, but not too close to the stitching.
- Pin the edging in place, but sew it with the embroidery foot on as the fabric cannot go into a hoop. Cut the net away from behind the edging.

zigzag following line of heavy weave of the lace

Curtain 2

- Pin lace shape, as explained on page 47, then place net in hoop with lace shape uppermost. As this lace is much finer than in Curtain 1, sew a single line of stitching carefully round the edge to hold it firmly in place, removing each pin as it comes. Then zigzag round the edge as in the illustration, ending with a few straight stitches.
- Cut away net from behind the shape.
- The single line of stitching can be omitted when you feel competent enough.

Above. Bella

Opposite. Motifs on net curtain

Agnus Dei

BELLA

Technique from Chapter 3, illustration on page 73.
Measurement of embroidery 48cm, 17in × 29cm, 11½in on a 5cm, 2in grid. For information on pattern transfer and enlargement see pages 53 and 54.

This design
Sewn on polyester/cotton using 50 machine embroidery thread.

Instructions
Use different colours top and bobbin except grey chest shading. Top tension as loose as possible because of the thick oversewing. Stitch width 0.

Technique
Bella looks very impressive, but is in fact *simple* to sew. Practically the only movement of the hoop is that described in the illustration. Try it on a spare hoop and see. If the work is to be stretched and mounted, see page 55.

- The stitches are quite long, so they catch the light and show up.
- Start at the tail and work towards the head to imitate the lie of the fur. Look at the way the fur grows on a cat's face. The eye was the last thing sewn, and it brought the cat to life.

Colour
The back of this work has large areas of solid colour, dark brown under the tail, orange across the back and shoulders, cream under the shirt front and whole front leg, and so on.

- Fill the bobbin and use till it runs out. The top colours must be changed often, as you can see. The bobbin colours need to show through, especially at the end of each run of stitching, to give the fur life.

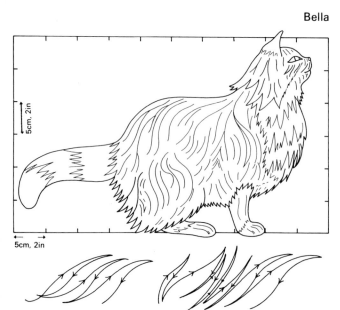

Bella

practise moving the hoop this way   simple stitching movement for the cat fur

Hints for your own design

For a black cat you would have a light colour in the bobbin to give the fur depth. The grey shading gives the white fur life.

If you are not a cat person, work a dog or some other furry animal. Imitate the way the coat lies, and look at the colour inside the coat. The technique used is very simple and the amount of such stitching involved in doing an animal is excellent practice.

AGNUS DEI

Techniques from Chapter 3, illustration on page 73.
Measurement of embroidery is 13.5cm, $5\frac{1}{4}$in, front hoof to tail, × 14.5cm, $5\frac{1}{4}$in, halo top to hoof. For information on pattern transfer and enlargement see pages 53 and 54.

This design

Sewn on sheeting, using DMC Fil Argent a broder, and 50 machine embroidery cotton in dark grey; Madeira thread in gold, silver and 300 pearl; ordinary sewing thread in dark brown.

Instructions

Important—check all tensions on practice hoop first, check them out of the hoop if the work is not to be stretched. If the work is to be mounted, see page 55.

Order of sewing:

Halo 300 pearl top and bobbin, top tension loose.

Furthest legs Fil Argent top, dark grey bobbin, top tension loose.

Main body, head, tail, and nearest legs: Fil Argent top, silver bobbin, top tensions: main body very loose, rest loose.

Hooves; leg, tail, chin and ear shading; eye nose and mouth; cross; halo outline: gold top and bobbin, top tension loose.

Emphasis lines on ears, chin, mouth, nose; eye: ordinary dark brown thread top and bobbin, top tension loose.

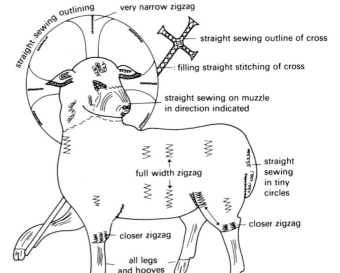

Agnus Dei

75

Hints for your own design

If you don't like the thicker Fil Argent a broder (or Fil Or), use the Madeira instead. If, no matter how loose your tensions are, it is still puckered a little, back the work with thin quilting wadding, and quilt round the design to take up the puckering.

FREDA GRAHAM'S GREETINGS CARDS

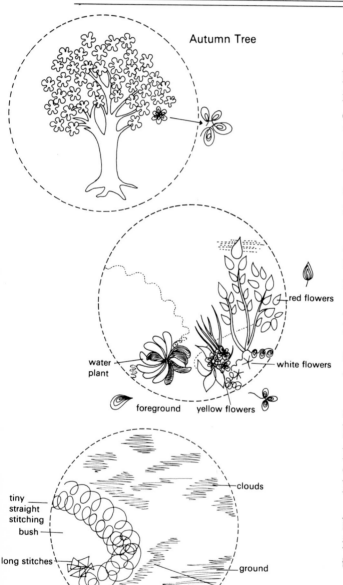

Techniques from Chapters 3 and 5. Measurement of circle $9\frac{1}{2}$cm, $3\frac{3}{4}$in. For information on pattern transfer and enlargement see Chapter 8.

Both embroideries were based mainly on simple movements of the hoop from side to side, up and down, or round in free or controlled circles. The designs are inserted into commercial card blanks.

Autumn Tree

Sew on Terylene worsted using 50 machine embroidery thread.

Instructions

Use the same thread top and bobbin, top tension normal to loose with stitch width 0—very narrow open zigzag.

Trunk—Green thread top and bobbin, open narrow zigzag, outline trunk and branches and fill in trunk as in colour plate. Change bobbin to white, sew one or two lines running up from trunk into higher branches.

Leaves—Bronze thread top and bobbin—sew in series of circles as in illustration. Change bobbin to white and touch up the odd leaf circlet.

Summer by the Beck
By kind permission of Freda Graham

Summer by the Beck
Sew on cotton linen-look fabric using 50
machine embroidery thread.

Instructions
Use the same thread top and bobbin with top tension loose to
tight and stitch width 0–full width.

Background Top tensions all normal to loose.

Clouds—white top and bobbin, blue top and white bobbin,
blue top and deep pink bobbin. Straight stitching side to side.

Ground—bronze top and white bobbin, straight stitching
side to side.

Water—black/grey variegated top and white bobbin.
Straight stitching side to side.

Bush—green top and white bobbin, straight stitching as in
illustration and some very long stitching, also indicated.

Foreground Tension as for background.

Leaves and stems—darker green top and white bobbin. Top

tensions normal to loose. Water plant wide zigzag all in same direction. The rest straight stitching as indicated in illustration.

Flowers—top tension tight as for whip stitch, water plant—bronze top and deep pink bobbin, sew as illustrated. Yellow flowers: yellow top and white bobbin, sew as illustrated. White flowers: white top and bobbin, mixture of small circles and star shapes. Red flowers: bright red top and deep pink bobbin, sew as illustrated.

Hints for your own design
Try your own simple mix of movements and colours in other designs. The white in the bobbin gives it a water-colour effect.

LITTLE DIRNDL AND APRON

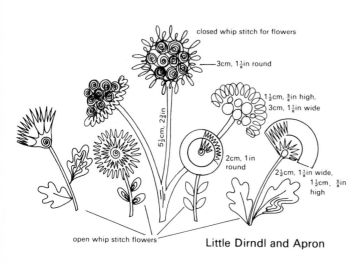

closed whip stitch for flowers

3cm, 1⅛in round

5½cm, 2¾in

1½cm, ⅝in high, 3cm, 1⅛in wide

2cm, 1in round

2½cm, 1⅛in wide, 1½cm, ⅝in high

open whip stitch flowers

Little Dirndl and Apron

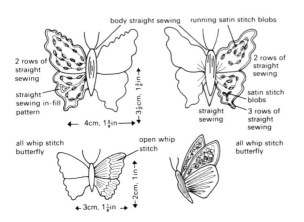

body straight sewing running satin stitch blobs

2 rows of straight sewing

straight sewing in-fill pattern

2 rows of straight sewing

satin stitch blobs

straight sewing

3 rows of straight sewing

3½cm, 1⅜in

← 4cm, 1⅝in →

all whip stitch butterfly

open whip stitch

all whip stitch butterfly

2cm, 1in

← 3cm, 1⅛in →

Techniques from Chapters 3 and 5, illustration on page 80.

Measurement of embroidery is 13cm, $5\frac{1}{8}$in × 8cm, $3\frac{1}{8}$in. For pattern transfer and enlargement, see pages 53 and 54.

This design
Sewn on minimum care polyester/cotton fabrics using variegated and plain 50 machine embroidery thread and ordinary sewing cotton.

Instructions
- Closed whip stitch flowers, use ordinary sewing cotton top, variegated machine embroidery thread bobbin with a tight top tension and stitch width at 0. Completely cover the top thread, sew as indicated in illustration, central spirals first, then petals.
- Open whip stitch flowers, use contrasting colours—ordinary sewing cotton top, plain embroidery thread bobbin, with a tight top tension and stitch width at 0. Colour of the bobbin thread stays

the same throughout each flower, although the top thread may change. See page 37 for technique used.

- Stems and leaves: Same thread top and bobbin, top tension loose with stitch width at 0. Outline stems and leaves and fill with straight stitching rows.
- All whip stitch butterfly: as for open whip stitch flowers.
- Larger butterflies: machine embroidery thread top and bobbin, top tension loose with stitch width at 0.

    Paler thread in bobbin throughout sewing on butterfly.

Hints for your own design

All the colours used in these embroideries are sweet pea colours. Choose a range of colours and stick to it for a more satisfactory design.

JOYCE WALKER'S DANDELIONS

Techniques from Chapter 3, illustration on page 81.

Measurement of embroidery is 15cm, 6in square. For information on pattern transfer and enlargement, see pages 53 and 54.

This design

Sewn on heavy polyester fine twill with 50 machine embroidery thread.

Instructions

Use the same thread top and bobbin with a loose top tension and stitch width 0—full width.

Stems and leaves—stems are sewn with straight stitching rows; outline leaves, indicate veins in contrasting colours and fill with close rows of straight stitching.

Buds—full width satin stitch as indicated.

Flowers—rows of half-width satin stitch on largest flower, in variegated cotton, less than half width for small flower and bud.

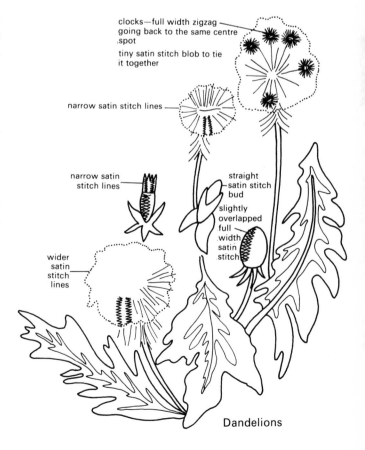

clocks—full width zigzag going back to the same centre spot

tiny satin stitch blob to tie it together

narrow satin stitch lines

narrow satin stitch lines

straight satin stitch bud

slightly overlapped full width satin stitch

wider satin stitch lines

Dandelions

Clock—brown clock lines first, there are about 19 of them on the original; a white clock at the end of each plus some extras, say about 8 or 9, not attached to anything to give lightness. Centre is without a clock.

This is a panel of a quilt and so is not mounted. However it would make a pretty picture. See page 55 for mounting instructions.

Hints for your own design

Wild flowers are lovely to embroider if you have a leaning in that direction. Ideally study them at first hand or look at books on wild flowers, or the countryside, or at calendars.

SARLA'S GARDEN

Techniques from Chapters 3 and 5, illustration on page 84. Overall scale of actual work 19cm, 7½in × 16.5cm, 6½in. For information on pattern transfer and enlargement, see pages 53 and 54.

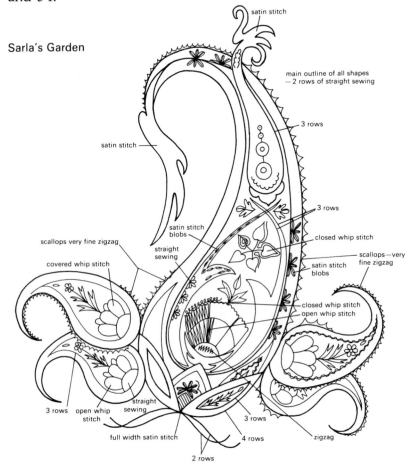

Sarla's Garden

satin stitch

main outline of all shapes — 2 rows of straight sewing

3 rows

satin stitch

3 rows

satin stitch blobs

closed whip stitch

scallops very fine zigzag

straight sewing

scallops—very fine zigzag

covered whip stitch

satin stitch blobs

closed whip stitch
open whip stitch

3 rows   open whip stitch   straight sewing

3 rows

zigzag

full width satin stitch

4 rows

2 rows

This design

Sewn on sheeting, using 50 machine embroidery thread and ordinary sewing cotton. *Always* try out all techniques on a practice hoop first.

Instructions

Use ordinary sewing cotton top, machine embroidery thread bobbin for whip stitch; machine embroidery thread top and bobbin for straight sewing and zigzag. Top tensions—tight for whip stitch, loose for other sewing with a stitch width from 0–full width.

- When tracing this design, only put in the main outlines. *Don't* include any details like scallop edging, the little leaves, satin stitch blobs etc, as you won't repeat them exactly. *Do* put in a few indication lines, like the centre stalk of leaves or one or two scallops to get you going and keep the work in place.

  Nobody is going to check your work against the picture in the book, so it doesn't matter if it is not an exact copy. Follow your own inclinations as you go along. If the work goes askew, just decide you meant to do it like that!

- Get some sort of order of sewing in your mind before you start. Wind your bobbins ready and don't be afraid to change your thread often, it only takes 10 seconds!

- Where you have to sew several rows of outline sewing, keep the stitches on the long side. Be very relaxed when sewing them and it will work beautifully—the occasional wiggle doesn't matter, or if it does, a bit of laborious unpicking is indicated.

Hints for your own design

The world is your oyster on this one! Choose a range of colours and stick to them. Make sure you have strong as well as pale colours, avoid having them all of the same intensity.

LIFE IN PROGRESS

Technique from Chapter 3, illustration on page 85.
Measurement of embroidery is 20cm, $7\frac{3}{4}$in × 28cm, 11in. For pattern transfer and enlargement, see pages 53 and 54.

This design

Sewn on sheeting, using 50 machine embroidery thread.

Instructions

Same thread top and bobbin with a loose top tension and stitch width at 0–half full width.

Always practice on a spare hoop before committing yourself and your fabric. Although there are only simple techniques used in this picture, it requires the greatest control, so, unless you are a person that does not give up easily, do one or two of the earlier projects first. If you don't fancy the stitching and shading of the cats, but want to do the notice, just sew the cat in outline and their faces, several times round.

The secret of the cats is trying to see them as three dimensional in your mind's eye, whilst you are sewing them, so that the shading 'talks' to you. Lighter thread in the bobbin adds light and lustre to the fur, dark thread in the bobbin adds depth and shading. The main outlines of shading are marked in the design, as is the lie of the fur. The little cat on 'Life' has cream in the bobbin when sewing her brown face to give it contrast. The gleam in the eyes is white.

- The serpentine pattern through the 'Life' letters is a very narrow satin stitch. You may find it easier to sew the word 'Life' with the foot and feed. 'In progress' is about half full width satin stitch.

Hints for your own design
If you are not a cat lover this won't be a winner! So find some books of dogs or other favourite animals or birds, and replace the cats. They'll need to be sewn in much the same way.

COUNTRY COTTAGE TEA COSY

This design
For the walls, use polycotton sheeting; for the roof, furnishing plush fabric; and black fabric for 4 windows, brown fabric for 2 doors, scraps of net and fabric for curtains. Use washable quilting as wadding and 50 machine embroidery thread; ordinary sewing cotton for walls and roof. You will also need narrow bias binding.

Instructions
Check the size of your pot before making the cosy. This was made to cover a 2-pint teapot. To bring the pattern pieces up to size, use a 1cm, $\frac{1}{2}$in grid using a centre line as indicated.

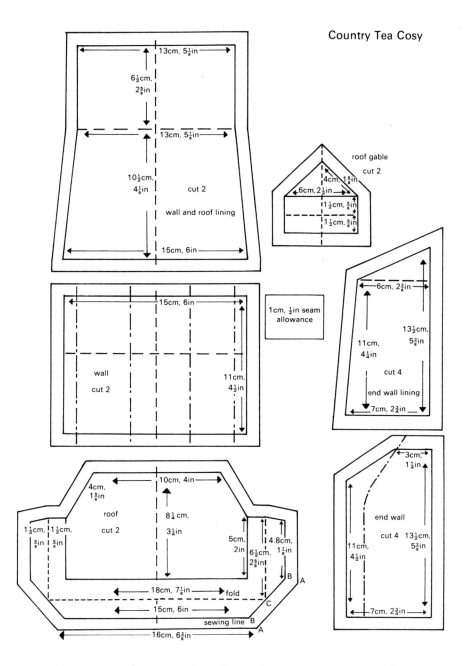

- Trace complete set of wall and lining pieces onto fabric.
- With the fabric not yet in hoop, use foot and feed. First, fold bias binding in half and sew 4 vertical strips on each main wall, then sew cross strip full width and end wall strips full width.
- Cut out black windows and brown doors, iron into place with Bondaweb.
- Pleat white net over each side of both windows of one wall, sew in place with straight stitching along the window edges, and trim. Repeat with curtain fabric for one window on other wall (diagram a).

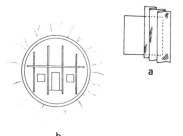

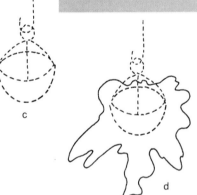

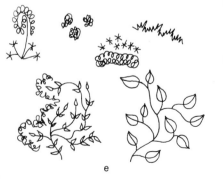

- Stretch the fabric in a hoop to hold (part of) one wall; remove foot and feed (diagram b).
- With dark grey top and pale grey bobbin, sew lattice in straight stitching over the complete window including curtains, on three windows.
- Sew details on doors, and house name (whatever is applicable).
- With foot and feed, satin stitch round all window frames, doors and step. Remove foot and feed.
- Hanging baskets: sew hook and basket outline (see detail), then greenery and flowers. By sewing the basket shape first, the flowers will sit right (diagrams c and d).
- Embroider formal flower beds for house front and more riotous beds for the back of house. But plan ahead; sew the flowers at the back of a bed first. Take the flowers over the lower sewing line to give a good edge. Sew over bias binding and windows. All the flowers in the picture were sewn with straight stitching. If necessary sew leaves then flowers on top (diagram e).

- Sew climbers of some sort, with or without frames, up the side walls. If you sew grass, be sure it goes over the sewing line, or it will start growing some way up a wall (diagram e)!

To construct roof Replace foot and feed.

- Sew both gables onto one roof piece; iron lightly with point of iron (diagram f)
- Join the other roof piece, sewing from centre outwards, iron (diagram g).
- Embroider thatch markings on roof. Full length straight stitching and long legged stitch. (This can be done with foot and feed) (see below).

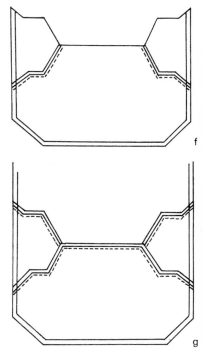

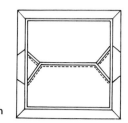

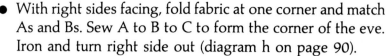

h

- With right sides facing, fold fabric at one corner and match As and Bs. Sew A to B to C to form the corner of the eve. Iron and turn right side out (diagram h on page 90).
- Cut a piece of wadding to fit the roof with the eves turned over. Attach by sewing carefully through roof centre seam.

To construct walls

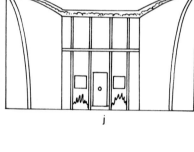

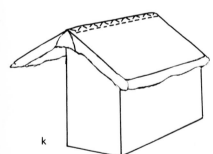

i

- Iron work on wrong side, and cut out all pieces, remembering seam allowance.
- *Sew an end wall to either end of a wall, repeat with linings. Press seams.
- Right sides facing, lay one set of lining onto one set of walls. Lay both onto wadding, lining uppermost.
- Sew from centre, through all thicknesses, along bottom edge and out to upper end wall. Sew in other direction (diagram i).
- Trim wadding round wall tops to match. Trim spare wadding from seam edges.
- Turn right sides out. Press sewn edges. Repeat from * with other set of walls (see diagram j).

To construct the rest

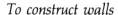

j

- Join one set of walls to roof. With right sides facing, sew through walls and wadding and edge of roof, mid-gable to mid-gable, along the sewing line from centre outwards. *Do not* sew through the lining. Repeat with other set of walls, and roof (diagram k).
- With roof wadding in place, sew round the eve close to the outside walls, with zipper foot (diagram l).
- Close the lining inside top of cosy then join end walls at top and bottom of opening by hand.
- Sew through corner seams 1.5cm, $\frac{5}{8}$in up, to hold the lower lining in place (diagram m).

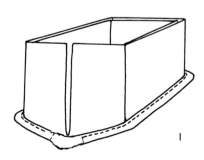

k

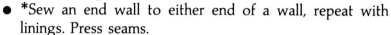

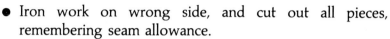

l

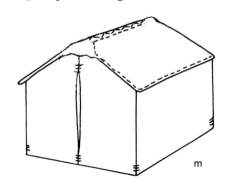

m

List of suppliers

The following shops sells DMC (D), Madeira (M) or Natesh (N) machine embroidery thread. Some of these shops do a postal service (PS). Water Soluble fabric (WSF). These are not the only shops to sell these threads, check the shops near to you and see if they do, too. They are in alphabetical county order including Greater London.

Suzanna's Secret, Berkeley Centre, Queens Road, Clifton, Bristol. (M)

The Workbasket, 38 High Street, Great Missenden, Bucks. 02406 3232 (D) (M)

Collingwood Crafts, 39a New Street, St. Neots, Cambs. 0480 77034 (D) (PS)

Hepatica, 82a Water Lane, Wilmslow, Cheshire. 0625 526622 (M) (PS)

Silken Strands, 33 Linksway, Gatley, Cheadle, Cheshire SK8 4LA. 061428 9108 (M) (N) (WSF) (PS only or by appointment)

Beldale Crafts, 121 Raby Rd, Hartlepool, Cleveland TS24 8DT. 0429 221972 (D) (M) (WSF) (PS only)

Hobby House, 3/4 Little Castle Street, Truro, Cornwall. (D)

Russells, 30 Castle St, Carlisle, Cumbria, CA3 8TP. 0228 43330 (D) (M) (WSF) (PS)

Ainsworth Sewing & Knitting Centre, 13 Beetwell St, Chesterfield, Derbyshire. (D)

Mary Allen, Wirksworth, Derbyshire DE4 4BN.

Hook & Eye, 2 Corn Exchange, Albert St, Derby. (M)

Strawberry Fabrics, Batworthy Mill Chagford, Devon. (D)

Hang it All, 1 White Lane, Barbican, Plymouth, Devon. (D)

Jane Willimott, Stone, Cornwood, Ivybridge, Devon PL21 9QY. (M) (PS only)

Busy Hands, 65A Fore Street, Bovey Tracey, Devon TQ13 9AB. (M)

The Sherborne Tapestry Centre, 1 Cheap St, Sherborne, Dorset DT9 3PT. 0935 815361 (D on request)

Franklins, 13a St Botolphs St, Colchester CO2 7DU. (D) (PS)

Regent Sewing Machines, 13 Station Lane, Hornchurch, Essex RM12 6JL. (M)

The Campden Needlecraft Centre, High St, Chipping Campden, Glos. 0386 840583 (D) (M) (N) (WSF) (PS)

Liberty, Regent Street, London W1. (D)

Woolhouse, 99 Chiswick High Rd, Chiswick London W4. (D)

Artisans, 22 High Street, Pinner, Middx. (D)

de Denne, 159 Kenton Rd, Kenton, Harrow, Middx HA3 0EU. (D) (M) (PS) (WSF)

Redburn Crafts, Squires Garden Centre, Halliford Rd, Upper Halliford, Shepperton, Middlesex TW17 8RU. 0730 67201 (M)

Barnyarns, Old Pitts Farm, Langrish, Petersfield, Hants GU32 1RQ. 0730 67201 (D) (M) (PS)

Pauline Deverell, 'Mylor', Church Hill, West End, Southampton, Hants. SO5 5AT (PS)

Alison's, 63 Hatfield Rd, St Albans, Herts, AL1 4JE. 0727 33738 (D limited choice) (PS)

Teazle Embroideries, 35 Boothferry Road, Hull HU3 6UAN. 0482 572531 (D) (M) (PS)

Singer Sewing Centre, 47 Paragon St, Hull. (D)

Pastimes, 93 High St, Hythe, Kent, CT21 5JH. (M)

Seale Needlecraft Centre, 97 Camden Rd, Tunbridge Wells, Kent. 0892 22445 (M) (PS).

Thread Bare, 5 Forester Drive, Fence, Burnley, Lancs BB12 9PG. 0282 601069 (M) (PS only) (WSF)

Wool 'N Things, 30 Kings Street, Sileby, Nr Loughborough, Leics LE12 7NA. (M)

Polly Peters Needle Craft Supplies, 13 Stourton Rd, Ainsdale, Stockport, Merseyside, PR8 3PL. (M)

The Voirrey Embroidery Centre, Brimstage Hall, Brimstage, Wirral, Merseyside L63 6JA. 051 342 3514 (M) (PS)

Jane's Pincushion, Wroxham Barns, Tunstead Rd, Hoveton, Norwich, NR12 8QU. (M)

Jane's Pincushion, North Lodge, Church Close, West Runton, Norfolk. (D)

The Handworker's Market, 18 Chapel Yard, Albert St, Holt, Norfolk. (D)

D. J. Hornsby, 149 High Street, Burton Latimer, Nr Kettering, Northants. (D)

The Calico Tree, 6 Alemouth Road, Hexham, Northumberland NE46 3PJ. 0434 602065 (Limited choice)

Nottingham Handicrafts Ltd, 17 Ludlow Hill Road, Melton Rd, West Bridgford, Nottingham NG2 6HD.

Craft Cottage, 33 Banbury Road, Kidlington, Oxon. (D)

Mollie Picken, The Old Post Office, Subford Gower, Banbury, Oxon OX15 5RT. (D)

Cat's Whiskers, 73 Temeside, Ludlow, Shropshire. (D)

OSA, 11 The Parade, St Mary's Place, Shrewsbury, Shropshire. (M)

Arts and Interiors, 48 Princess St, Yeovil, Somerset. 0935 77790 (Limited choice)

J.M Needlecraft, Lychgate House, High St, Pattingham, Nr Wolverhampton, Staffordshire WV6 8BQ. 0902 700597 (M) (D) (WSF) (PS)

The Needlecraft Shop, 4 Smallgate, Beccles, Suffolk, NR34 9QQ. 0502 713543 (D) (PS)

Needle & Thread, 80 High St, Horsell, Woking, Surrey GU21 4SZ. 048 62 60059 (N) (M) (PS)

The Spiders Web, 37 Hill House Close, Turners Hill, Crawley, W. Sussex RH10 4YY. (M) (PS only)

Sutton Needlecraft Centre, 40 Birmingham Rd, Sutton Coldfield, W. Midlands B72 1QQ. 021 355 1731 (D Limited choice) (WSF) (PS)

Mace and Nairn, 89 Crane Street, Salisbury, Wilts. SP1 2PY. (D) (M) (WSF) (PS)

Touchwood Crafts, 15 Warminster Road, Westbury, Wilts. (D)

Woodseats Sewing Machines, 37 Cambridge St, Sheffield, S. Yorks. (D)

Howden's Sewing machines, James Gate, Bradford, W. Yorks. (D)

Sebalace, Waterloo Mill, Howden Rd, Silsden, W. Yorks BD20 0HA. 0535 55885 (D) (PS)

Whaleys Ltd, Harris Court, Great Horton, W. Yorks BD7 4EQ. 0274 576718 (WSF) (PS)

The Craft House, 23 Bar St, Scarborough, N. Yorks. (D)

Crimple Craft Ltd, 107 Cold Bath Rd, Harrogate, N. Yorks HG2 0NU. 0423 526426 (M) (PS)

Lalla Thomas, 415 Abergele Rd, Old Colwyn, Colwyn Bay LL29 9PR Clwyd, Wales. (M)

Gerrard's Wools, 23 High Street, Cardigan, Dyfed, Wales. (D)

Knitters' & Sewers' Word, 21 Park St, Swansea, Glam, Wales. (D)

Gavenny Fabrics, Chapel Farm Cottage, Pentre Rd, Abergavenny, Gwent, Wales. (D)

Christine Riley, 53 Barclay Street, Stonehaven, Kincardineshire, AB3 2AR, Scotland. 0569 63238 (D) (PS)

The Embroidery Shop, 51 William St, Edinburgh EH3 7LW, Scotland. 031 225 8642 (D) (M) (PS)

Jenny 'a Things, 3 Lainshaw St, Stewarton, Kilmarnock, Ayr, Scotland KY3 5BY. (D) (M)

Templetons, Mill Street, Ayr, Scotland. (D)
Madeira Threads (UK) Ltd, Ryder House, Back Lane, Boroughbridge, N. Yorks YO5 9AT. 09012 3555
DMC Threads, Dunlicraft Ltd, Pullman Road, Wigston, Leicester LE8 2DY. 0533 811040

For a comprehensive list of suppliers in the U.S.A. see *The Complete Book of Machine Embroidery*, Robbie Fanning (in book list). These addresses were correct when going to press.

Bibliography

Books about, or that include, embroidery on the sewing machine.

CARROLL Mary (Ed.) *Making Needlecraft Landscapes.* (See especially Margaret Adler's Laburnum Arch), David and Charles, 1986.

CLUCAS Joy *The New Machine Embroidery.* David and Charles, 1987.

COLEMAN Anne *The Creative Sewing Machine.* Batsford, 1979.

FANNING Robbie and Tony *The Complete Book of Machine Embroidery.* Chilton Book Company, Radnor, Pennsylvania, 19089, U.S.A. 1986.

HUBBARD Liz *Gutermann Thread Painting.* Search Press, 1985.

McNEILL Moyra *Machine Embroidery,* Lace and See-Through Techniques. Batsford 1985.

WARREN Verina *Landscape in Embroidery.* Batsford, 1986.

Books with ideas for designs.

BAIN George *Celtic Art.* The methods of construction. Constable, reprinted 1986.

BANBURY Giseal and DEWAR Angela *Embroidery for Fashion.* Batsford, 1985.

CHAPMAN Suzanne E. *Historical Floral and Animal Designs for Embroiderers and Craftsmen.* Dover, 1977.

MESSENT Jan *Embroidery and Nature.* Batsford, 1980.

— — *Embroidery and Animals.* Batsford, 1984.

— — *Embroidery and Architecture.* Batsford, 1985.

— — *The Embroiderers Work Book.* Batsford, 1988.

ORMESSON Linda *Jacobean Iron-on Transfer Patterns.* Dover, 1978.

Acknowledgements

I would like to express my thanks:

To Ruth Bawden and to Marge Hurley, who offered themselves and their time as my guinea pigs during the writing of this book, and whom I cannot thank enough for all their carefulness, thought and enthusiam.

To Freda Graham, who first got me working creatively on the sewing machine, and is my sounding board and a very great help in trouble.

To Joy Clucas, my teacher.

To Jean Curl, of the Hertfordshire Federation of Women's Institutes who, having strongly encouraged the National Federation of Women's Institutes on my behalf to set a Home Economics Certificate in Machine Embroidery, then strongly encouraged me to take it! This set me on my enjoyable WI career in teaching and demonstrating my craft.

To Ann Morris and her WI Royal Show Committee, whose invitation in 1986 to demonstrate in the WI pavilion made me aware of the need for this book to be written.

I express my further thanks to Freda Graham and Joy Clucas, and to my student Joyce Walker, for allowing their work to be used in this book.

And to my husband Ivor, my constant encouragement and support, who during the preparation of this book has had to type most of his own letters and work, and has willingly turned a blind eye to such things as dust and hurriedly prepared meals!

The publishers would like to extend
their special thanks to Jil Shipley for her
drawings and Steve Tanner for his enthusiasm
with the photography.